A travel guide of a very special
his wife and two small children,
Japan. He reports on his many encounters with Japanese culture and ways of thinking, as well as adventurous, bizarre and beautiful experiences in the land of the rising sun. Whether it's killer hornets, love hotels, office workers in closets, remote-controlled bathtubs or deep-fried gourmet asparagus ends, Willem Spelten has experienced and tried it all.
With wit, charm, and a great respect for Japanese culture, he helps readers participate in that culture through many valuable tips that will prepare any traveler for their own visit to Japan.

This book is not only for those interested in Japan, but for everyone who wants to immerse themselves in foreign cultures and be entertained at the same time. Japan will certainly be at the top of your travel wish list afterwards.

Willem Spelten, born in 1979, has worked as a journalist and press officer in Stuttgart, Vienna and Tokyo for the past 25 years. He and his wife are united not only by their love for their twin sons, but also by an interest in Asia that has grown over many years. The family currently lives in Luxembourg, where this book was written during many long weekend nights.

Willem Spelten

Hidden Japan

A journey to the most fascinating, exciting and sometimes disturbing country on earth

Editing: Dr. Carola Carstens, Humza Ahmad
Translation: Humza Ahmad

Reach the author: willem@hidden-japan-book.com

ISBN 978-99987-967-2-0

2nd edition 2024

To my Nomiguys and all the friends we made in Japan

Content

Travel and accommodation in Japan

The food in Japan

Family and Friendship in Japan

Work and work culture in Japan

How to behave in Japan - best possible

The Japanese language

Bonus for those who want to learn even more about Japan

Foreword

During my first short business trips to Japan, I sometimes felt like an orc who had mistakenly stumbled into elf country. I stood aghast as streams of people flowed elegantly, through the urban landscape about all around me, functioning in a highly complex world while I could just stand and watch.

But from day one, I was fascinated by this country. It was a land of contradictions: overwhelmingly loud and impressively quiet; was home to huge crowds and yet harbored great loneliness; celebrated absolute perfection and accepted constant decay. Japan was so beautiful, yet so completely different from what I was familiar with that I despaired of it and yet couldn't get enough.

A few years later, my family of four packed all our belongings in a 40-foot sea container and moved to Tokyo. With the move, we plunged head-first into Japanese culture, cuisine and the fascinating cosmos of the approximately one hundred and twenty million people in this island kingdom.

Our sons, who were two and a half years old at the time, didn't really care where in the world their cribs were. My wife and I, however, naturally wanted to prepare ourselves as well as possible from afar. We had some expectations, shaped by popular portrayals of Japan, but often these expectations simply turned out to be wrong. No guidebook could prepare us for all that we were about to experience in Japan.

Japan is not a country full of robots and highly mechanized everything. On the contrary, a good part of office communications are still done by fax. Japanese apartments are only very rarely harmonious refuges furnished according to Feng Shui and tidied up according to Marie Kondo. For the most part, they are crammed small apartments in which there is almost always too little space for the inhabitants.

Inherent contradictions are what make many countries fascinating and exciting. Nowhere does this fit better for me than in Japan, where appearance and reality, saving face and actual emotional state, and strict rules and actual interpretations are often wildly divergent.

On journeys across the country, in the office and in everyday family life, but above all in many conversations with Japanese friends and acquaintances, our picture of Japan became broader and broader, our understanding better and our impressions deeper. And that's what I want to share in this book to whet your appetite for the real and often hidden Japan. To arouse your curiosity, and to offer you lots of ideas and starting points for your very own discoveries in the land of the rising sun.

At the same time, this book is certainly not complete, and it is highly subjective. It was not my intention, nor do I presume, to completely depict Japanese culture here in its fullness and complexity. This is not a scholarly work, but an enthusiastic, respectful and entertaining journey through the most fascinating, exciting and sometimes disturbing country that I've had the good fortune to explore.

Tokyo

Our way to Japan and Tokyo

My relationship with Japan began sometime in the 2010s, early in the morning, with the landing of a Lufthansa plane at Narita International Airport. Bleary-eyed, I got into a cab after thirteen hours in the air, some restless sleep on the plane, and brief immigration formalities. I spent my first hour on Japanese soil in the back seat of an ancient yet very comfortable Toyota Crown, my “throne” in the backseat covered in white lace. It smelled a bit like my grandmother's living room, and the driver, fittingly, was about grandma’s age. His words were limited to "Thank you" throughout the ride, but he confidently chauffeured me to the center of Tokyo.

At first, the highway led across fields and farmland, then the houses crowded closer and closer together, slowly piling up into apartment blocks and finally into high-rises. My fatigue evaporated, and I gazed out, fascinated, as a city built up kilometer by kilometer in front of the cab’s window. Finally, we drove over the iconic Rainbow Bridge. I was suddenly surrounded by a dense urban jungle: Tokyo.

Below me, the water of Tokyo Bay; to the left, the open sea; but ahead of me, only skyscrapers as far as the eye could see. The sun was just rising, the endless glass skyscrapers to the west reflected the light over Tokyo Bay, and I couldn't take my eyes off of all of it. The panorama in front of and beside me seemed so much larger than New York, much denser than Beijing, and much more urban than London. It was unlike any other city I had visited before. But most importantly, the skyline was not dominated by a few standout buildings, as is so often the case in modern urban landscapes. Instead, the two landmark towers, Tokyo Tower and Tokyo Skytree, rather unobtrusively decorated the huge, glistening, homogeneous mass of buildings. And I could hardly wait to dive into it.

That first morning I fell head over heels in love with Tokyo and Japan. And I admit, it was a very superficial love affair at the time.

The character of this city, and really the country on a whole were almost completely unknown to me. I just liked what I saw and the promise of adventure. But isn't that the beginning of many great love stories?

I was to stay in Tokyo for only a few days, and with all the work I had to do it was difficult to experience anything of the city, let alone its inhabitants. On that first, short visit it was the little things that captivated me.

There was the tranquility. The largest city in the world is a quiet one. Nobody honks, at any time. Traffic on eight-lane roads at rush hour just flowed along, almost silently. The Yurikamome Line elevated train, running from central Shinbashi to the artificial island of Odaiba, rolled on rubber wheels instead of the usual steel wheels of normal trains, and thus disturbed the residents along its route much less than the screeching and squealing equivalents in many other cities. The people around me on the street, in trains and in the offices where I worked were also quiet. No one was talking on the phone on platforms or in trains – in fact, no one was talking loudly at all. Everything was simply quiet and peaceful.

Later I learned that there are definitely other sides to Tokyo and Japan. But the first impression of this country was very close to my idea of a tea ceremony: quiet, concentrated, distinguished and a just a bit magical.

This first visit had me hooked. I started traveling to Japan more and more often, sometimes for short visits to tradeshows, sometimes for longer projects in Tokyo. Visit by visit, I dared to dive a little deeper into the city and its culture. But it was a complicated love affair. Behind every door I opened, there was both a new discovery and a new puzzle. How did the queues in front of restaurants work, where guests were called by name seemingly at random by the host? Why did the few characters that had been identified as particularly important and that I then memorized appear so rarely in the city? Why did none of the inhabitants of this seemingly cosmopolitan city seem to know English when spoken to?

Fortunately for me, my wife's good friend Nina had fallen in love with Japan while still in college, had lived and worked there for many years, and helped answer some of these questions for me. In front of the restaurants, you sign up on a waiting list with your name and seating requirements. After that, the host assigns your seats. On the issues I faced with reading important things, there are actually three different writing scripts in Japanese. All three are used in parallel as well as in conjunction with each other, so simply memorizing three characters in one of the scripts doesn't help much. And the English problem: all middle and high school students in Japan take classes in English. However, with a strong focus on reading and grammar, practical skills in listening, speaking or writing are not practiced. This causes most Japanese adults to be reluctant to and more often than not simply unable to understand or speak English with any level of proficiency.

After all these trips, I gushed on and on to my wife about how endlessly fascinating Japan was, and we decided to visit the country together in 2015. We wanted to mimic those oft-ridiculed Japanese tourists from the '80s, who blasted through the entire European continent over the course of a 5-day vacation. We gave ourselves a little more time, but still covered as much of Japan as possible. We spent three whole weeks exploring a good part of the large northern island of Hokkaido on bicycles, roaming mainly on foot through Tokyo and Kyoto, and touring the tropical island of Okinawa in the south by rental car.

After this trip, we shared the impression that we had been immersed in a culture that offered much more than ours. In all our previous encounters with other countries and peoples, we had always appreciated what was different, but also looked forward to being back home. Sometimes we wished for more peace and quiet, sometimes for more cleanliness, were disappointed by the cuisine or had to worry a lot about our safety. But in Japan, everything just fit.

Back in Germany, the people suddenly seemed a bit loud and unkempt in comparison, ourselves included. We returned to an astonishing amount of garbage lying around and found that the food was not only served in incredibly large portions, but also seemed quite monotonous to us. Now my wife was on the same page as me: We wanted to go back, and not just for our next holiday, but we wanted to live in Japan for some time.

We were fortunate that in 2019 the opportunity arose for me to take up a job in Japan and to bring my family along. My wife and I discussed it, we slept on it for two nights, and then I applied.

The confirmation of my posting to Japan was followed by many preparations that warrant a separate book entirely. Besides organizing the move and handling formalities, the most important thing for us was to get off to a good start as a family. We diligently began learning Japanese, which turned out to be even more difficult and complex than we had expected. Our twin sons were two and a half years old at the time and we also wanted to prepare them for the move, or as well as you could prepare toddlers for an international move. Night after night, we looked at picture books from Japan with them, practiced a few words like *konnichiwa* and *arigato* together, and explained to the boys on a globe where Germany is and where Japan is.

And then came the big day. With ten suitcases, a twin stroller and two car seats in tow, me, my wife, and our two lovely boys boarded a plane to Tokyo.

Unlike my very first trip, we arrived not early in the morning, but at noon. We were welcomed by a bright blue winter sky and by our friend Nina and her daughter holding a big "Welcome to Japan" sign. The start to our adventure could not have been better. The four of us then drove to our apartment building in Ota Ward, one of the southern districts of Tokyo, where our family life in Japan began.

The whole world in one city

From day one, living in Tokyo was a completely different experience than just visiting Tokyo. We felt like we had gone to see a show, and suddenly found ourselves cast on our very own roles on stage. We lived our daily lives by performing our very own play together with all the other residents of this city.

To be honest, I can't claim to have comprehensively penetrated Tokyo. You simply cannot know or explore the Japanese capital in its entirety. Tokyo is at once dense, exciting, large, tangled, confusing, detailed, run-down, ugly, charming, tempting and, for a fairly typical European expat like me, even exotic. This diversity is endless, as something is constantly being torn down, rebuilt, reopened or closed. From my first business trip to my last day as a resident of Tokyo, the city continued to transform at breakneck speed.

In order to properly understand this fascinating and confusing diversity, one must keep in mind that Tokyo exists in two dimensions. Not only in the lateral plane (how we normally conceptualize geography), but also in the vertical plane.

We liked to spend evenings in a building near our home that we found extremely convenient. There was a small barbecue restaurant on the eighth floor, a very cozy cocktail bar on the sixth floor, and then karaoke rooms from the seventh down to the second floor. So we could start with dinner at 7 p.m. at the top, then hop down two floors for the innkeeper to provide us with some liquid courage that we then used at karaoke, again one floor below, where we were completely outclassed by the singing skills of our Japanese friends, who were just bang on.

This verticality of the city has always been a great challenge for me because more often than not you just can't see what's hidden inside a building as you walk by. So while walking along the street when you walk in, you will usually find a small sign on the outside façade of each building listing what you can find on each floor. The next problem is that these signs are usually written in kanji -

the Japanese characters adopted from Chinese, which are the most difficult (and for me usually impossible) to read. There are, however, exceptions. For every ten Japanese signs there are two with English subtitles, which is already a kind of invitation in and of itself for foreigners like us. In such cases, we often just took the spiral staircase or the elevator to the floor in question. This is how we discovered some of the most beautiful and our absolute favorite places in Japan. I wholeheartedly recommend this strategy.

Of course, Google Maps and similar digital tools also help to orient oneself to some extent in the orchard of signs. However, you quickly realize that even excellent software runs into problems when ten bars share a single building. A good friend of mine, who emigrated from Ukraine to Japan years ago and started a family there, worked with hundreds of other programmers at Google Japan on the localization of Google Maps. He explained to me that in Tokyo there is simply too much information in too few square meters. As a result, the software giant is able to map a good six hundred square kilometers of densely populated urban space, but it struggles to display a wide variety of bars and restaurants from the second basement level all the way up to the eighth or tenth floor of a skyscraper that is only a few meters wide.

But even with limited software support, you can embark on the Tokyo adventure without a care in the world. At worst, you might get lost - but there's very little danger lurking around you in the Japanese capital, which is one of the safest cities in the world. So you can look for exactly what you're in the mood for and you can always find something new. Even within a few hundred meters of our house in a residential area, far from all the city's hotspots, we regularly discovered new things.

A café that only offers Sardinian pastries? No problem. A deli for dogs that sells fifteen different kinds of freshly prepared dog food every day? Gladly. Brothels that look like subway cars so you can live out your commuter train fantasies there? Yes, Tokyo has that too. We stumbled upon an exciting combination at a store in our neighborhood that sold mountain bikes and vinyl records side by side. This pairing was apparently not understood by many people besides me, because the store was also closed after a few months. One of my personal favorites luckily survived longer, a very nice specialty store for rare books and freshly tapped craft beers. A good read and a tasty drink, what more could you want?

And the city does not disappoint in the search for superlatives. The best pizza in the world can be found in Tokyo, from a repeat winner of the annual Neapolitan pizza competition. The best baguette is also available, baked by last year's winner of the "Mondial du Pain" in Paris. Both winners, by the way, are not immigrants, but home-grown Japanese perfectionists.

We already knew this from our visits here, but as residents it became even more apparent and important: knowing Japanese helps. In normal shopping at the supermarket, in getting to know the neighbors, and simply everywhere where you want to go deeper into the exciting world beyond the global expat community, working knowledge of and facility in communicating in Japanese is key. In the beginning, we were always helped by our friend Nina and her family, who took us under their wing after our move and accompanied us, for example, on our first big shopping trip to a supermarket. This helped us a lot when we arrived and so we lost that initial fear of doing something wrong. After that, I was lucky enough to learn some rough, somehow functional "basic Japanese" to survive in the office. A Japanese colleague once said to me, fortunately in English, "Willem-san, it's fascinating how you can actually order food and ask for directions with your primitive pub Japanese". So much for Japanese politeness... Fortunately, both my wife's talent for the language and her eagerness to learn were much greater than mine. She was so motivated to learn both the spoken and written language that she enrolled in a language school where she studied with a motley crew of men married to Japanese women, computer programmers and embassy staff. Following her first year of studies, she had cleared the first three of the five officially recognized levels of Japanese and thus became a great communication bridge for our family, especially in rural areas.

What nevertheless remained a challenge was ordering in restaurants. There are several reasons for this. For one, menus, especially in small restaurants, are often handwritten. This makes the characters even harder to read than they already are, and even automatic translators can very rarely decipher handwritten Japanese. If you then ask the host, of course every fish, every exotic vegetable and almost every dish in itself has in turn a name that you do not know. And even if you are very lucky and understand the ingredients, it is usually difficult to interpret the preparation method correctly. Therefore, the only thing that helps here is to simply try it out. Sometimes we laughed out loud when instead of the expected cooked spinach came a raw seaweed salad. Or the supposedly vegetarian tofu was covered by a large fish. Nevertheless, it always tasted good, and when we made a particularly good discovery, we got into the habit of having the host write down the correct name so that we could confidently order it directly in the future.

Regardless of whether you know Japanese or have to communicate with your hands and feet, food is a huge part of Japan's appeal and uniqueness. Here you should really have no fear of contact when you are traveling somewhere in the country. The quality, uniqueness and variety of the cuisine is simply extraordinary. You really have to eat and drink your way through the country to fully experience Japan.

Why does everyone look so good here?

As a tourist, I usually left the house relaxed and rested around 10 or 11 o'clock in the morning with the subway into the city, usually traveling together with students and retirees while walking on the road. An eclectic mix, but not appreciably different from what you might see anywhere else in the world.

However, as working member of Japanese society, starting the office day at 8 in the morning was something completely different.

On my first day of work in Tokyo, I walked to the nearest subway station without giving it much thought. I didn't have abnormal expectations for my traveling companions on public transit: I had been to Japan often enough to know that you don't always see green-haired manga girls in fishnet tights or boyband-inspired bodybuilders while outside. Just a normal mix of commuters was what I thought I would find. Instead, as I entered the train station, I found myself surrounded by a stream of people in uniform business suits of black and white. It felt like the entire city population surrounding me wore dark suits, dark skirts, or dark school uniforms with white shirts and blouses.

I suddenly felt very out of place. My suit was blue. I was wider and taller than everyone else. Nobody else had blonde hair on this platform. And my tie was not dark like 99.9 percent of the ties on this platform, but in an obvious fit of insanity, I had reached for a green tie that morning. I was clearly the only outsider for as far as anyone could see, and I longed to merge with the homogeneous mass around me. Most likely no one noticed me that morning, since my fellow travelers were for the most part absorbed in their cell phones, but I felt as if I had accidentally confused a wedding with a theme party. It was as if I was the only one wearing a rainbow jacket and jester's cap on this first trip to the office.

They say New York is a city that never sleeps. Tokyo doesn't sleep very deeply either, but the metropolis ticks like clockwork. In many respects. The clockwork beats of the metro and the Shinkansen are the obvious pulse. Beneath that, there's still a dull, pervading bass note. These are the working hours in the high-rise office buildings as well as the parallel start of school lessons. They control a seemingly endless stream of office workers, the so-called "salarymen," and students. Around 6 a.m. in the very distant suburbs and then from 8 a.m. in Tokyo itself, their stream floods the entire transportation infrastructure. Millions of people travel from home to their respective destinations for the start of classes at 8:30 and the start of work between 8 and 9. And the vast majority of these people, as described, wear suits or uniforms. It is an army of very well-dressed, well-groomed people that pours all over the city. In the vast majority of cases, all the travelers also have black hair. The latter for obvious genetic reasons, but there is another reason: many schools and some employers forbid any other hair color. Try a little blond or even the green mentioned at the beginning? Expulsion from school. These strict rules continue into working life. Some banks or large corporations accept only black hair in their departments with customer contact. In some institutions, Japanese people with foreign parents who might naturally have lighter hair are reportedly even required to dye their hair black on company orders.

As for school uniforms, for young children they are only required by private schools, then at high schools for almost all students in Japan. However, there are very, very many private schools in Japan and especially in Tokyo. Therefore, the proportion of even very young girls in sailor dresses or boys as young as six years old in uniforms strongly reminiscent of Prussian traditions and in many other types of very neat, demurely austere school clothes in the morning is extremely high.

As soon as students arrive at school, their shiny black shoes are removed outside the classroom, and they enter the room in slippers. This nice habit is often continued later in the office. High-heeled pumps or tight lace-up shoes are gladly parked under the desk here to be exchanged with Birkenstocks or other sandals.

With all the uniformity in public life, the biggest and most colorful bright spot in the subway are women in kimono. Not necessarily in the morning at 8 o'clock, but from noon and into the night, there are always occasions when people put on these traditional and beautiful silk dresses. This can be for many different reasons, from a family gathering to a photo shoot with loved ones. But whatever the occasion, kimonos add so much color and grace to the hustle and bustle of the metro that I was always happy to spot someone dressed in one.

If you want to try on a kimono yourself and have photos of it - no problem. Kimono dressing and photo sessions can be organized very easily everywhere in Japan, and usually not as a simple tourist rip-off. Every one of the country's 125 million inhabitants takes photos in traditional clothing at least a few times in their lives. In the vast majority of cases, Japanese people will also use the rentable clothing of a nearby photo studio for this purpose. On Japanese Instagram accounts, as a cover photo on LINE (the local WhatsApp equivalent) and with most Japanese families I know, wedding photos and family pictures with everyone in traditional Japanese clothes hang on the wall at home. Arrangements for these photo sessions range from simple to highly complex. You can get wrapped in a one-size fits all kimono for a 10-minute photo session in front of a floral wallpaper, or you can invest in a huge package deal with many hours of makeup, hairdressing and dressing in a valuable historical kimono, in which you are then photographed among trees and on the bridges of a local garden. For this reason, you can see signs in many public gardens that prohibit professional photography or photography with a tripod in general - the rush of nobly dressed families blocking lines of sights and lining up outside teahouses is simply too great.

But what about our green-haired manga fans, do they only exist in the cinema? No, of course not. If you don't already know where to look for them, you have to search a little harder to find individually styled or dressed people in Tokyo. The dress and styles of Tokyoites differ quite significantly by neighborhood and even by street. If you like it a little younger and more colorful, look around in the inner-city area best in Shibuya and Harajuku. Here there are many music bars, trendy stores and significantly more creative people than in many other areas of the city. The very wild days of the 70s and 80s are over here, too, and former music clubs are increasingly being displaced by shopping malls, but it's still a lively, young hotspot that's fairly easy for tourists to get to and wander through.

Two peculiarities of Japanese fashion should be mentioned here. One is the use of lace and tulle. In girls' and women's fashion, both fabrics are found in places where I didn't even know that fabric could be decoratively attached. For example, on the cuffs of socks. Where smooth fabric protrudes from shoes in the rest of the world, tulle is always peeking out in Japan. It looks a bit as if someone had been at a princess's birthday party and had forgotten to take off all parts of the costume.

The other peculiarity of the Japanese fashion world is an unimaginable density of secondhand stores. Before my time in Japan, I would never have imagined that the cleanliness-loving Japanese would love secondhand of all things. In fact, in hardly any other industrialized country are there as many secondhand stores as in Japan, from very individualized boutiques selling exclusively luxury brands to entire department stores with fashion starting at a hundred yen, or less than a euro.

The market leader in the second-hand trade, the Off Group, alone operates over one thousand stores throughout the country. These stores range in size from perhaps two hundred square meters in an expensive city center location, to multi-story shopping centers many thousands of square meters with H&M-sized clothing departments on major arterial roads. Here you can buy everything you can imagine. From used books to used golf equipment and surfboards to discarded notebooks and cameras.

In the context of fashion, the countless second-hand markets are also an important distribution point for status symbols. Almost new bags and belts from major luxury brands such as Louis Vuitton or Prada are brought here at the change of season by wealthy people who want to make room for pieces from the new collection. So, their six-month-old handbag quickly finds new owners for about 80 percent of its former price. They keep the bag for perhaps two to three years - and then take it to the second-hand store in their neighborhood. There the good piece, by now with a few small scratches, goes over the counter for the third time for about fifty percent less than the original price. And so on and so forth.

Since people in Japan are very careful about their wardrobe and never (really never) put handbags on the bare floor in restaurants, for example, but rather in specially provided baskets, this passing on of very well-kept goods works over a long period of time and thus ensures a "democratization" of status symbols. Which in turn are very important for social status and on some occasions are simply considered indispensable. In my extended circle of friends with very down-to-earth or even creatively independent Japanese women, every lady had at least one handbag from Chanel. Perhaps there were other brands for other occasions, but a bag from Chanel had to be part of the collection. It was simply the right thing to do. And, for example, there was absolutely no question of wearing a Chanel bag on important official occasions, such as the children's first day at school. In black. Those who were really brave chose a red or colorful model. But that was almost as daring as my green tie on my first day at work.

The best metro in the world

My morning routine in Tokyo was then quickly settled. Put on a black suit, a dark tie, and off I went on foot in the direction of the subway. First past a major intersection, then through a very beautiful avenue with old gingko trees and finally across the pedestrian square in front of my station, where people coming from different directions formed a kind of wedge to then disappear in unison through the entrance gates. Like almost everyone else, I confidently pulled my smartphone over the chip reader of the entrance portal, which acknowledged with a beep that I had activated a valid prepaid card loaded onto my phone. Unhindered, I was able to hurry into the station concourse, hang a U-turn to the left, take the escalator to the platform, and there board my train bound for the office.

And that was it, simple, efficient and consistent. You can't do much wrong getting in and out of the trains in Tokyo. I managed to mess up on my first week of work anyway...

Every train line in Tokyo has its own platform. This rules out many mistakes from the outset. What I didn't realize was that there may be many different types of trains on the same line: Local, Express, Commuter Express, Limited Express, Special Express, Airport Limited – the possibilities are endless. As for my train line, Local trains stop at every station, Express trains only stop at selected stations, and the Commuter Express train stops at the very major hubs on the line.

I had a slow start to the day that morning and left a few minutes later than normal I followed my usual route, stood on the platform and simply waited for the next train, as I had done before. Since I felt safe on this route, I didn't confirm the connection on Google Maps, and I didn't take the time to decipher the large display panels on the platform in detail. At first glance, it said the same as always.

I was surprised to find an absolutely packed train pull onto the platform. Much fuller even than my normally densely packed train.

I thought that, well, maybe something happened this morning and even more people than usual pressed themselves into the train... So with that I pressed myself together with the other passengers and began my morning commute daydreams.

After a little while it dawned on my that my train was not only moving very fast, but it had hardly stopped. In my head, I usually always counted the 7 stations to the destination, but we had only stopped twice and were already traveling for quite a while. I was sweating bullets as I came to the realization that I was traveling in the completely wrong direction. A quick check of my phone confirmed that I was almost out of Tokyo again! Instead of my local train, I had boarded the Commuter Express, which stopped at my station a few minutes later, and it was now speeding me through the countryside.

Slightly panicked and definitely running a decent delay for my start to the office day, I got off at the next stop, changed platforms, reassured myself several times on my cell phone that I had the right connection, and then, better safe than sorry, took the safest, slowest possible route towards my office on a connecting train and two slow Local trains.

To save yourself a similar mishap, there are two rules: First, you should always use a good public transport navigation software, such as Google Maps, and do pay attention to the route details! The fine print matters here. The routing through the public transport in Tokyo is fantastic with Google Maps, and as long as you pay attention (like I didn't) you will always catch the right train.

Second, delve a little into the displays on the platforms. They are much easier to understand than one might think at first glance. At almost all stations, the type of service for each train is displayed in both Japanese and English. And when Google sends you to a local train, there's no way you're jumping on the express that stops on the same track just a minute before.

If there are no multilingual display boards and your phone is not cooperating, there is a good old-fashioned printed timetable somewhere on every platform that shows the stops of all train types in English and with easy-to-understand graphics. On the arriving trains, it is also always clearly stated above the windshield in English what type of train it is and to where the train is going.

By the way, it is worth getting on a train in Tokyo at the very front car, right behind the driver's compartment at least once. He is separated from his passengers by a large window and can therefore be easily observed while doing his job. You'll notice a special treat: Japanese train drivers practice various hand movements in order to always perform their tasks correctly. This means that the train driver must perform certain checks every time certain things happen, for example when the train starts, when it passes special signals, when it enters stations and on many other occasions. To ensure that he never forgets a click, a glance or the pulling of a lever, all drivers are drilled for many months on strict movement choreographies. Unfortunately, all of these occasions and all of these motions never quite made sense to me.

What does this choreography look like? Before the train starts, for example, the driver slowly raises both hands from his lap to eye level. At the same time, his gaze follows his hands, which means that he first sees the train track directly in front of the train and then his gaze wanders further and further into the distance. To check that there are no people or objects there. Then he points with his fingers from his eyes to the two outside mirrors (not sure why, as he's in no danger of being overtaken...) and clearly turns his head there. After that, he flies his hands over various displays, clearly counting along with his fingers and pointing at some hidden numbers. Finally, he puts both white-gloved hands on his accelerator lever and, accompanied by a slight nod of the head, carefully gives power. All this ritual is completed with sacred seriousness and at every single station.

Another nice observation I made while riding the trains in Tokyo: At some stations, Local trains wait to be overtaken by an Express. At these stations, Local drivers apparently have a rule that they must get some fresh air. I once had some fun and timed this process: the driver moves to the window, opens it, happily inhales and exhales, and after exactly sixty seconds returns to his control lever. At least on my rail line, I was able to set my watch to this peculiar but refreshing occurrence. There are a lot of people in Japan who take their jobs incredibly seriously, but train conductors are right up there with the best of them for me.

I have already described that it is important to take the right type of train when riding the metro. It is just as important to leave from the correct exit once at your destination station. In large stations like Shibuya, there are dozens of exits. All are numbered separately, and underground there are large maps that show where which exit is located and where it leads. However, the labels are not always in English either. Therefore, the same applies here: Google Maps and similar apps are the traveler's best friend. If you specify exactly where on the surface you want to go, Google always suggests the most suitable exit. And that's the one you should take. It's much easier to move around underground than in Tokyo's street canyons. Exit thirteen, which branches off underground just a few meters from exit fourteen, can be many minutes' walk from the other subway exit when on the surface.

Of course, I also had to learn this lesson first, during an early morning attempt to take a special train from Shinjuku out to the countryside with the family. Note that Shinjuku Station is one of the largest and busiest train stations in the world, with over 200 exits. Shinjuku Station is so big and has so many exits that "Shinjuku West Exit" has an entirely separate station named after it!

Instead of taking the escalator into the station concourse from the underground subway destination stop as expected, we suddenly found ourselves standing in a city park. I was about as dumbfounded as my family was looking at me. My overconfidence as a supposedly "experienced" Tokyoite led us to try to find the right way above ground, rather than diving back into the orderly underground channels of the station. I lugged our two suitcases, my wife a large trekking backpack, and the two of us together with our whining children through the park in the morning in the supposed direction of Shinjuku Station. It was a singular ordeal. We got completely lost, the station didn't appear at all for a long time. By the time Shinjuku Station finally entered our field of view, we found ourselves hopelessly separated from it by a multi-level bus and taxi terminal with no footpaths and thus no way to walk directly to the station. So we had to trudge around the bus terminal to finally reach the doors of the train station. All in all, we were exhausted, sweaty and late, and only reached the platform after half an hour of walking. It would have been so much easier to stay underground for a little longer and search for the correct exit.

What you should also avoid, besides choosing the wrong exit, is using a lot of trains in weekday commuter traffic. On my normal office route, the crowds were limited, which was fortunate. But between about 7:30 and 9:30 every weekday morning the majority of Tokyo's public transit system turns into the world's largest vice squeezing its passengers inch by inch. Fainting spells are common, especially during the summer, on some lines during rush hour, and some even get cracked ribs. Thousands and thousands of perfectly dressed passengers, in their immaculate suits and uniforms, stream on and off the trains, squeezing in mercilessly.

One morning, following my first few weeks in Tokyo, rather than making my way to the office, I found myself heading toward the central district of Roppongi. At my home station, I was still able to board the Toyoko line towards the city center in a reasonably relaxed manner, but a few stops later, the train was already bursting with people. It was impossible for anyone on the train to use a cell phone anymore or even raise their arms - we were simply a huge can full of people pressed together, and I could feel myself starting to feel sick. Thanks to my height, I could see out of the mass of people in the train car, but the physical pressure, the high temperature and the lack of oxygen were extreme stressors.

Although our train was completely overcrowded, at every stop what seemed like hundreds of people waited on the platform to enter our sardine can, but only four to five were able to take a step in. They were unable to press themselves fully into the car under their own power, so they waited until the doors closed. The hydraulic system then took care of further compression. The five additional passengers were then pressed into the interior of the train and all of us Commuter Express sardines were now even closer together.

Often the doors had trouble closing completely when we did this. I'm not sure if there was a safety device that limited the pressure, but it didn't seem that way to me. But time and again, the portals failed to close completely because a lady's handbag or a briefcase of the newcomers who had just been pressed inside got caught in it. In these cases, two white-gloved gentlemen appeared on the platform. The train door opened again a little bit, the two gentlemen took position, pushed the disturbing bag inside and then forcefully pushed the sliding doors closed.

Completely aghast, I watched this procedure several times, the entire time being hardly able to breath. All the windows were fogged up, because the air conditioning was completely overwhelmed with the crowds. I noticed how my head began to tingle and how my eyes slowly went black. With the courage of desperation, I somehow pushed myself forward and out of the train at the next stop, stumbled onto the platform and sat down on a bench for ten minutes to regain my composure. It was still before 8 a.m., but I was already exhausted from the day. Fortunately, I was traveling with enough of a buffer that I could walk the rest of the way. That ended up being about an hour's walk from Naka-Meguro to Roppongi, but anything was better than getting back on another train.

As a result, I never rode the main lines at rush hour again. I rescheduled appointments, used my own car, or took a cab. Presumably one can get used to the crowds, as apparently all those other users of these trains could. But I was so affected by my near faint that I had absolutely no desire for further training.

Throwaway houses and capitalist urbanism

In purely building terms, many Japanese rural villages and towns are quite unsightly - not to mention ugly. Instead of romantic wooden houses with Japanese gardens, beautiful city centers with large pedestrian zones and a diverse array of well-kept museums, one usually finds cubes of plywood and rusty metal covered with thin stone slabs or tiles, countless faceless shopping centers outside the city center and an all in all rather chaotic and loveless-looking collection of buildings.

What happened here? As always, there are various factors that interact. And of course there are exceptions, the most famous being Kyoto as a beautifully preserved and maintained historic city.

As a rule, however, neither houses nor neighborhoods in Japan grow as old as the parts of Kyoto that are worth seeing. This is due, primarily, to natural disasters and the high risk of fire. About a hundred years ago, for example, seventy to eighty percent of Tokyo was completely destroyed in the great Kanto earthquake and the resulting fires on September 1, 1923. A good twenty years later, the relatively newly rebuilt city again was demolished in the US Air Force's firebombings of World War II, in which about fifty percent of the city was burned to the ground.

The second very important factor is that an old building in Japan is simply not considered to be of great value unless it is a temple or of outstanding historical significance. Historic preservation for private buildings is virtually unknown, and there is very little public desire to preserve the old. While the age of a person contributes quite significantly to its high status and is seen as something very valuable, age for a building usually just means that it will soon be demolished. The standard useful life for residential and even commercial real estate in Japan is therefore quite short: one generation or around thirty years. And since the useful life is so limited, people do not invest unnecessarily in preservation. The valuable thing in Japan is the land. The building on it serves only a temporary purpose and is removed and replaced at will for new purposes.

This throwaway mentality in buildings means that houses are not built to a very high standard from the outset. Walls of new Japanese buildings are currently no thicker than perhaps twenty centimeters, despite recent slight increases in thermal insulation requirements. The shell of a large apartment building is delivered by a single truck, and consists of simple wooden beams and plywood, which are stapled together within two to three days. Thanks to a nice stone-look cladding or plastering the walls, it ends up looking impressive and neat, but after a few years the first cracks start to form, after twenty years everything creaks and cracks, and after thirty years it's over.

We ourselves lived in Tokyo in a fairly young house that was just ten years old. But even after this short time, almost every component of the building services failed at least once, and our energy costs for heating and cooling were eight times what we paid in Germany.

In addition to the cheap construction method and the low interest in investing sustainably in preservation, there is another reason for these often unsightly buildings: taxes. In Japan, property taxes are very high, but they are eight times higher for an undeveloped property than for a developed one. So it makes a lot of sense from the owner's point of view to let a vacant house deteriorate rather than demolish it. If you take a walk through the peripheral, more residential districts of Tokyo and look around, you will see many examples of how this tax-saving model is being used diligently. In more attractive real estate markets in Tokyo, it sometimes takes only weeks, rarely a year, for a vacant house to be demolished. In the countryside, however, houses are very often left for decades, falling into ruin right in the middle of villages and small towns.

Traditionally, Japanese cities are often built according to the "castle town" principle, including the center of historic Tokyo. In feudal Japanese cities, the castle was located in the center, around it were the residences of the nobility (yes, those were the well-known samurai), followed by craftsmen and merchants. And around it were large temple complexes. The samurai quarters consisted of houses and gardens, connected by irregular streets and alleys.

According to reports, these paths were intentionally so tangled that attackers not only got lost but could also be greeted with a sword behind many corners and bends. The principle of this labyrinthine wayfinding has not been changed in old urban areas until today, often even continued.

In contrast, there are some very "Western", boulevard-like street layouts - these were generally conceived during the Meiji Restoration between 1860 and 1880, such as the Ginza district in Tokyo, which was designed on the drawing board at the time and is now the most well-known and oft-frequented shopping district. Here, London, Paris and Berlin were the inspiration. But the rule in Japan is rather a chaotic, confusing routing full of curves and intersections, which does not make it easy for a tourist to grasp or understand a city.

In the 20th century, a completely new determinant of urban life came into play, which still shapes the cityscape today: the local, regional and nation-spanning train lines. In Japan, many train and subway lines were built by various private companies, and some people and families on the side of these companies, as well as the city government officials entrusted with planning work and awarding concessions, became very, very rich in the following decades. The close link between the state, the economy and the common good is a peculiarity of Japanese society that is difficult to understand for many foreigners. This may also be due to the fact that, according to my Japanese friends, the yakuza, or Japanese mafia is heavily involved in a few select sectors of the Japanese economy, including construction and real estate development.

But back to the rail lines. While the core of the Tokyo subway system was built by two state-owned companies (one of which has since been semi-privatized), the lines leading into the more remote areas of the city and the surrounding countryside belong to eleven different operating companies. Imagine boarding a bus from New

York City to Boston, and that bus is run by several different companies at once. While you are sitting in the very same bus, different operators with different fare systems are responsible for select parts of your voyage. At the end of the trip, luckily, there is only one invoice to be paid. But depending on the actual routing of your bus, the very same trip can cost different amounts of money that will then be shared among the different operators.

In the 20th century, the companies operating these railroad lines bought wide strips of land with state licenses, massive backing from the central government and, by all accounts, often with great pressure on unwilling residents. The tracks were laid in the middle of these strips. To the right, left and all around were built houses. And infrastructure. And entire cities. All privately owned.

To illustrate this with an actual example, Tokyu Corporation is a railroad company that is about one hundred years old. To this day, it operates various rail lines in southern Tokyo, primarily between Shibuya and Yokohama. However, Tokyu Corporation does not only operate these train lines, but currently consists of over five hundred real estate and urban development companies. Along their routes, they operate and own hospitals, housing complexes, shopping malls and cinemas. One of the largest security services in Japan once evolved from the Tokyu Corporation Railway Police. Tokyo's best-known hardware store is called Tokyu Hands. Tokyu Store is popular grocery chain. There are Tokyu Group hotels all over the country, and even the daycare centers along the railroad lines are run by Tokyu.

I mention Tokyu here as only one example. There are many other conglomerates and massive developers having no connection to the transit sector, which have made it their business to develop Japanese cities, with the obvious aim of maximizing sustainable profit from the areas they once developed with the backing of city governments. Urban development as an overall concept, the coherent design of public space, even something like visual splicing lines in the city, do not appear in these plans. Instead, each company optimizes its own environment.

As a result, large building complexes such as the shopping/office/residential project "Roppongi Hills" are impressive, but self-contained and completely self-sufficiently functioning urban districts. Although they can be easily reached by train, they are inconvenient to leave on foot in the direction of the surrounding construction projects of competitors.

Even if this building practice is not good for the cityscape in Japan - the protagonists are doing extremely well with it. Taikichiro Mori, the founder of the successful Japanese Mori real estate group, was the richest person in the world until his death in 1993.

Pachinko, the officially non-existent game of chance

Almost everywhere in Tokyo, during a city walk lasting more than half an hour, you will at some point hear the incredible noise of a pachinko parlor. In every major shopping street and around many metro stops, hundreds, sometimes thousands, of gambling machines drone behind sliding doors covered with privacy film. And in these machines, in turn, thousands and thousands of small metal balls shoot back and forth, accompanied by an infernal soundtrack.

My childhood in Germany also included slot machines. Two or three of them hung on the bar of our local pizzeria. Every now and then, one of these machines would try to draw attention to itself with a restrained but incessant melody. It didn't bother me much. In a pachinko hall, however, every single machine is continuously making music and flashing with countless LEDs. The visual environment is nothing but obnoxiously blinking effects and rotating lights. What's more, each machine has at least one, often two or three, integrated screens that also flash, blink and pay homage to some theme - Sailor Moon, the latest Marvel blockbuster, or a Japanese boy band. All the machines combine to create a deafening racket, a completely overwhelming and wholly unwelcome sensory experience. Anyone who can sit here with their eyes open for longer than a minute is definitely not at risk of epilepsy.

But since pachinko is so Japanese and so ubiquitous with about thirty million regular players, it's a must-see spectacle. From early in the morning until late at night, sometimes around the clock, they can indulge in the game. An estimated three hundred thousand people work in Japan's pachinko industry, and the industry's sales reportedly account for over five percent of Japan's gross national product. According to an analysis by Fortune magazine, the profits from Japanese pachinko are higher than the profits of casinos in Las Vegas and Macau combined. This success has come at a social price. In 2014, nine percent of Japan's male population was found to be addicted to gambling.

Since most readers of this book will probably only visit Japan for a limited time, I think the risk of a strong pachinko addiction is rather low, and a little guide on how to play pachinko is in order.

In principle, it makes sense to have the process explained to you on site. In a corner, often to the left of the entrance, there is a kind of checkout area. There you simply speak to the next employee in English and ask for help. The person you speak to may not know English, but unlike many other places in Japan, there is almost always an employee at Pachinko who speaks English and is supposed to take care of foreign customers. And the colleague at the cash register who has just been spoken to immediately calls him to the foreign customer via the house radio.

With the English-speaking supervisor organized in this way, you then choose any machine. Here you can choose any theme that appeals to you. The basic functions of all machines are the same, it's just a question of whether you'd rather be cheered on by cartoon heroes or a boy band or whatever such thing while playing.

Now you put a 1000-yen bill into the machine and off you go. In pachinko, you buy small metal balls for your money. Usually these cost five yen per ball. So the thousand yen lets two hundred small marble-sized balls rattle into a sort of collection basin at the bottom of the machine. Next to it, you turn a small dial with your right hand - this controls the speed with which the balls are then automatically shot upwards into the machine. This is reminiscent of the good old pinball machine, where you also shoot the ball into the playing field at the beginning. In Pachinko, however, the player has no influence whatsoever once the ball has been shot - the metal marble rolls down through a field of nails and buttons, each contact with an obstacle causes a random change of direction. At the bottom, the marble disappears into a funnel without a sound. Or it may hit some special exits on its way, assuming some luck. In this case, it provides points, plus points, bonus points, multiplier points or the much sought-after "Fire Mode", in which the machine virtually explodes visually and acoustically as it provides plenty of bonus points with each shot ball.

The game itself is basically not strategic at all and can be downright boring. The right hand can only control whether the balls are shot faster or slower into the nail field to then find their way down. The left hand rests or feeds the player drinks when needed. That's all you can do. However, if you get involved with this and give up trying to put any ambition into the perfect (yet unmanageable) shot, with a little luck you can experience an incredible show.

In my second game, I somehow managed to activate the aforementioned Fire Mode. My already loud device then began to really outdo itself. The music got even louder, entire movie scenes suddenly appeared on the screen instead of the previous short animations, a large blinking tower of flashing plastic flames actually emerged from the top of my gaming device, and my Japanese neighbors interrupted their games to stand by me. Very excitedly, they explained to me with hands and feet that I now had to very quickly pot as many balls as possible into a newly appeared hole. And so, I turned my dial to the stop and sank one ball after the other into the brightly flashing bonus hole, and each of them increased my account balance by five yen. My slot machine was in absolute panic mode by now, honking and cheering and shaking, causing more and more spectators to gather around me. And I still didn't know what I was supposed to do - except stoically fire as many steel balls as possible.

At some point, the spectacle was over, my friendly neighbors patted me appreciatively on the shoulders and I had made a good ten thousand yen from the initial thousand yen bet. Judging by the fireworks in front of me, a million yen might have been more appropriate. But well, at least the stake tenfold and still had fun, that was also something.

I pressed the red button for "Service", a minute later the English-speaking employee was standing with me again. I explained that I wanted to leave, he put a card into the machine and saved my account balance on it. With the card, I then went to the cash registers where I had already stood at the very beginning.

But if you think you can pocket your winnings at these cash registers, you are mistaken. Gambling with cash winnings is prohibited in Japan. The country with the highest density of gambling halls in the world does not allow cash winnings in gambling because of the addictive effect. But Japan would not be Japan if there were not an elegant and face-saving detour to respect this law and still turn over many billions of euros in the gambling industry.

The trick here: In the Pachinko Hall there are only non-cash prizes. Namely, small consolation prizes and big special prizes. The machine said that I had won 10,240 yen, and for that, I now got a small gold bar of one gram at the cash register, which was the non-cash prize worth about ten thousand yen. And for two hundred and forty yen I was allowed to take another can of Red Bull, two chocolate bars and a lighter.

You can plaster the natural goods with which you get paid your small change as you like. The gold bar, however, you now have to carry out of the pachinko establishment. Always in the immediate vicinity, but in a separate building, there is a specialized gold dealer for each pachinko arcade. Who exclusively trades gold bars from the nearby pachinko supplier at fixed prices. For a bar weighing one gram you get here, you guessed it, exactly ten thousand yen in cash.

And so, the law is satisfied. The player does not win money, but a non-cash prize. The gold dealer is, of course, completely independent of the casino. The desire to play is not encouraged (not in cash anyway), and all parties are satisfied (technically).

Nightlife and Adult Entertainment

Tokyo has some of the best clubs in the world, especially if you like electronic music and hip-hop. In and of itself, a good club in Tokyo looks no different than in any other major city in the world. There are several floors, some bars and a lot of light, laser and sound technology. What makes Tokyo so special are the guests. It's just incredibly pleasant to party with Japanese people.

This starts at the entrance, which is often supervised by frighteningly large men with surprisingly many tattoos (and this in Japan, where visible tattoos are near-universally frowned upon), but is friendly and polite. There is no jostling, you stand relaxed in a long row and are surrounded by good-humored people who politely keep a little distance from each other.

After that, the party goes on until breakfast. And if a whole group of newly arrived foreign bachelors on a trip to Japan doesn't get lost on the dance floor, no one gets danced on and no one gets picked on during the whole night. It is simply a top party, without stress.

The best way to find out which club is hot and which is not is to visit the city. Trends change quickly, as do the owners and concepts of many establishments. And just as quickly as new houses are built, new locations are constantly springing up in the city. For men, most clubs cost between fifteen and thirty euros admission, for women little to nothing, you should plan accordingly. And much more common than in the West are lounges, VIP lounges and super VIP lounges, which means that often all or at least all central seating must be reserved and paid for separately, or in some cases come with very sporty minimum consumption costs.

What makes Japan's nightlife, other than the discos, completely different from most countries in the world are the more specialized clubs and establishments for men. And although for once I can't draw completely on my own field research here, I can't help but describe this very special universe. For me, it is emblematic in various respects of several peculiarities of Japan that can hardly be better explained by any other example.

Let's start with the hostess clubs. These are mentioned in many guidebooks, but it is never clearly described what they actually are and what happens there. The name sounds like a cheap whorehouse, but the vast majority of hostess bars are not so. Nor are they high-class brothels. You meet women there, but not for sex. You meet women there to talk to them. There really is nothing more to the basic premise than that. Hostess clubs provide encounters for cultivated conversation with an attractive counterpart who offers you closeness, attention, recognition and entertainment, which has been part of Japanese culture for centuries, and was most famously practiced by geishas from the 17th century onward.

Hostess clubs come in a wide variety of price ranges, and the price decides in which ambience you find yourself, how exclusive the circle of other guests is and how attractive the hostesses are. By the way, there are also quite a few host clubs, where ladies go for evening entertainment.

But let's stay with the better-known hostess clubs. This is where you can go in the evening to meet your favorite hostess, for example. If you have established a good personal relationship, she will also have time for you. If there is a guest with a better relationship, unfortunately you have to wait. Building such a relationship takes time and money. The hostesses want to drink with you in the club, and in doing so, collect a commission on their sales. But they also like gifts and delicious food.

Hostesses thus also like to go out to dinner with good guests before the club officially opens, for which they must of course be invited. I sat in Tokyo again and again in very good restaurants, where I discovered one or two couples with enormous age difference next to us. These mismatched couples almost always start dinner very early, around 6 p.m., and then pay as early as 8:30 and take a cab to the associated hostess club. The mama-san, the (often female) boss of a hostess club, wants to see her ladies back in her own store with the customers punctually at 9 pm so that the hostesses are drinking there, not in the restaurant.

I was lucky enough to meet the mama-san of a very established hostess club in person through friends. She told me that every now and then, of course, a lady does fall in love with a guest. But that was unprofessional and completely contrary to the spirit of the system. Because then it becomes difficult for the lady to work with other guests, and the regular guest suddenly prefers to sit with her on the sofa at home rather than at the mama-san's counter.

If you have earned a good status in a hostess club, you can of course bring guests there as if it were an "exclusive" living room. This is a standard expected by many customers at higher management levels and in sales in Japanese companies, so managers and successful salespeople can hardly avoid earning a certain status in a hostess club near their office. If, as a host, you then take your business partners to a prestigious hostess club after a good meal and are greeted there honorably by the mama-san in person, the customers know that their counterpart is a respected business partner.

Incidentally, understanding of how hostess clubs work is limited not only among most tourists, but also among international companies. Many non-Japanese corporations explicitly prohibit all forms of "adult entertainment" at company expense in their hospitality rules. And that's what "hostess club" sounds like, which can lead to big problems with expense reports, audits and compliance checks. The unofficial solution to this problem is that many established clubs offer different billing forms to their guests. Entirely correct with the name of the club itself on the letterhead, or alternatively with the name and logo of a real-life, innocuous restaurant nearby. This offer is also reportedly used by many a husband who does not want to account for four-hundred-euro whiskey bills at home.

I know from one of America's largest industrial corporations that their compliance department wanted to get to the bottom of the many hostess club invoices from their Japanese branch in great detail. So, two auditors from Boston were sent to Japan to spend three months reviewing hostess clubs and creating a "whitelist" of approved establishments for future business events. The Japanese colleague who accompanied the two Americans as a local consultant during this three-month journey through nearly a hundred hostess clubs in the country once told me over dinner that it had been the three greatest months of his life.

Things gets even more fascinating when you turn away from the hostess clubs and look at sex for sale. To start, commercial sex has been banned in Japan since 1956. Sounds progressive, no? The fathers of this law thought so too. Unfortunately, they were surprised by the enormous need and high demand for such services. At the same time, various interest groups, above all organized crime, began massive lobbying against this very modern, women's rights-oriented legislation. As a result, Japan found extremely creative ways to organize around the very progressive law in a face-saving manner, which means living with without having to repeal it.

Initially, Japanese courts determined that prostitution described only vaginal intercourse. This made all other forms of intercourse legal again, and oral sex in particular has since been offered virtually "on the go" in some red-light districts.

But now there were still many customers who demanded exactly the one forbidden form of prostitution. As a result, the judiciary determined that prostitution was only vaginal intercourse between two people who did not love each other. Conversely, this logically meant that people in love could have as much intercourse as they wanted. Since then, in simple terms, the following happens in so-called soaplands or health clubs: A man visits this establishment either to get a massage (health club) or to get washed (soapland). He pays for this service. Now he meets the lady who will treat him today. Spontaneously, both fall in love with each other - and have sex. After a certain time, which, by the way, correlates with the price for washing or massaging, the two realize that they don't love each other after all. And they separate again. The man leaves the establishment, and the lady can fall in love again.

Since this procedure is actually used and is hardly comprehensible for uninitiated foreigners, many soaplands or health clubs are reportedly only accessible to Japanese patrons. In addition, the image of foreign men is said to be not particularly positive. Ladies don't like to fall in love with them because they are often perceived as disproportionately rough and big. And Japanese customers are not fans of establishments that also serve foreign guests, because they are unanimously considered unkempt. Therefore, I assume that most of my readers will not be able to verify my descriptions. However, I have reproduced them according to credible reports from three Japanese acquaintances - so what I have described should be quite close to reality.

By the way, in some places the right to operate sex work is tied to buildings, almost like municipal zoning rules. The problem in Japan is that the right is actually attached to the building itself. If you tear it down, the license expires. That's why there's a saying in Japan that nothing is as dangerous as sex in a whorehouse during an earthquake. Because the houses have been the same for seventy years. True, the walls are fancy, the electrics are new, and at first glance everything may seem nice and modern. But while the buildings in the neighborhood have been demolished again and again and rebuilt to be earthquake-proof according to the current state of the art, these brothels are still completely from the 1950s in terms of construction. Thus, sex for sale in Japan actually seems to pose even more risks to individual health than the act itself.

The hidden wonders of the capital

Tokyo is one big wonder, and the city's greatest appeal comes precisely from the fact that it does not concentrate a few overwhelming highlights in its city center - but wants to be discovered street by street and neighborhood by neighborhood.

Admittedly, this is difficult to do during a short stay. Especially since one is so overwhelmed during the first visit to the city, that one hardly dares to go right into the thick of life during the first few days.

So here are my recommendations for some special Tokyo impressions. In each of the recommended stops I'll reproduce some observations that I have described elsewhere in the book.

At the same time, each recommended excursion serves to experience things unlike anywhere else in the world - and hopefully offer even more unforgettable Japan moments.

1. Wild jungle and a temple with a waterfall

Todoroki Ravine Park, via Todoroki Station

Just one hundred years ago, Tokyo was crisscrossed by numerous rivers and canals. Almost all of them were artificially placed below ground level to avoid flooding, reduce insects - and maximize urban space. Today, there is only one wild gorge left in urbanized Tokyo: Todoroki Ravine Park.

From the Todoroki train station, it's just a short walk down a flight of steps from the bright, noisy and, in summer, blisteringly hot city to a quiet, almost enchanted river valley with slightly cooler air, little light, overwhelmingly tall trees and a tranquilly flowing river in its midst.

It is unbelievable how powerfully nature proliferates here directly next to an asphalt desert and blocks of houses to completely take over the environment of the visitor. One expects at any time to be suddenly surrounded by a horde of monkeys, and yet one was just sitting in the subway.

You can't do much wrong in the gorge and just follow the course downstream. The whole path is only about a kilometer long, so you can't get lost. But there is a lot to discover, even away from the jungle with all its flowers, trees and birds.

Two highlights here: Just before the end of the valley, you reach a waterfall that marks the entrance to a temple area. Here you'll find a small tea house where you can drink a bowl of matcha and eat something. Then you climb up many, many steps and reach a large, very beautiful temple, the Todoroki Fudosan. This offers everything a visitor could wish for: beautiful buildings; a great location; ample opportunities to buy prayer sticks or incense - and a clean restroom facility. The temple appears so surprisingly when you climb the steps and is so picturesquely located that you feel more like Indiana Jones on a treasure hunt than a visitor to the world's largest city arriving by public transport.

If you then return to the valley along one of several paths, you will find a large garden gate a little further downstream. If you pass through it, you can now climb up again on the opposite side of the slope from the temple. This time, however, not on steps, but on curved paths through a simple Japanese garden.

Once at the top, a large meadow opens up. The heart of the small but very pretty Todoroki Ravine Park. Here you can take a seat on the terrace in a small, unmanaged but publicly accessible teahouse and polish off the drinks or snacks you've brought with you. And a rare highlight in Tokyo: You are allowed to sit or lie down anywhere on the lawn.

We have had some very nice picnics up here with friends as it offers a pleasant breather after exploring the gorge and temple. Afterwards, you can either stroll straight out of the park onto the main road and then back to the train or take the path through the gorge again in the opposite direction. This choice means another round of stair climbing at the end, but in return you can soak up some wilderness and birdsong before the big city swallows you up again.

2. Perfect gift shopping, space for reading and beautiful rooftop gardens with views of Mt. Fuji

Futakotamagawa Tsutaya Electrics, via Futako-Tamagawa Station

Tsutaya is a DVD and bookstore chain that has over a thousand outlets all over Japan. Most of these stores are nothing special and not particularly worth visiting without a very good knowledge of Japanese - English-language books and DVDs are either scant or simply not carried.

The situation is quite different with some of the flagship stores of this successful chain, however. Tsutaya Bookstore in Daikanyama is a spacious architectural masterpiece in a green setting that has translated traditional Japanese architectural principles into a very beautiful, classy bookstore in the form of three large bungalows. Even a bit more special is Tsutaya Electrics, a very large concept store in the Futako Tamagawa Rise shopping area. Futako Tamagawa is a comfortable Tokyo suburb across the river from neighboring Kawasaki, with lots of new high rises filled with young families.

So why do I recommend traveling here from the exciting downtown districts? There are two reasons: the store itself and the shopping center in which it is located.

Let's start with the center. Most of the stores here are more or less interchangeable. But the rooftop gardens are special. Since 2001, Tokyo's building code has required buildings with flat roofs larger than one thousand square meters to have gardens planted atop. The primary purpose of this is to reduce temperatures in the city, since the air above heated concrete or even bitumen surfaces often heats up to 140 degrees Fahrenheit in the summer. This effect does not occur above a lawn. At the same time, habitat for animals and insects should be created, as well as recreational areas for the urban population. Access to these roof terraces is also almost always free of charge.

As a result, very beautiful roof gardens have sprung up in the city center in recent years, and many buildings now advertise the beds, forests and fields on their roofs. Increasingly, large trees are being planted so close to the facades that even from the street one can clearly see the various greened floors.

At Futako Tamagawa Rise, the art of green roofs can be seen particularly well, as there are a large number of buildings of different heights here, and all of them have flat, green roofs. At these lofty heights you can even find playgrounds, a large kitchen garden where children can watch the gardeners grow vegetables, a pond with fish, a river course and more, all connected by bridges and elevators. Very impressive when you consider that such areas used to just lie fallow, scorching in the sun. A special highlight at the Rise is that the highest garden offers a long viewing terrace with a view of Mount Fuji. It's a great place to sit in the evening, drink a beer that you are free to bring with you, and watch the sun slowly sink behind Fuji's perfectly curved silhouette.

Amongst all the rather interchangeable stores in the Rise, you find Tsutaya Electrics. I'd dare to guess that this outlet was simply built to memorialize the Tsutaya brand, and not to make money. The concept of this shopping temple, completely furnished in Japanese wood, is to colorfully mix a huge bookstore with various interior design and electronics stores. You walk through aisles lined with bookshelves, only to suddenly turn right into a world full of wooden toys for children or to find yourself in an Apple store. You can pick up books and magazines everywhere, take a seat on one of countless designer chairs, a wall bench or at a small table and browse. In addition, there is an ongoing coffee supply from a Starbucks in the basement, which fits seamlessly between an e-bike store and giant potted plants. Every plant has a price tag; everything in this store is at once decoration, part of the concept, and merchandise.

In addition to international books and a really gigantic selection of international magazines, this store has very nice things that you will probably never need, but that can wonderfully remind you of your time in Tokyo and Japan. Japanese stationery and papers, many modern kitchen gadgets, knives, home textiles and porcelains "Made in Japan" want to be discovered and taken away here. All, of course, at prices that aren't exactly cheap.

Nevertheless, I can only recommend a trip here if you want to have an experience of "Contemporary Japan" - and without other tourists.

3. Countless Japanese people with mouse ears

Tokyo Disneyland, via Maihama Station

"I'm not going to fly all the way to Japan just to spend a day at Disneyland!" is something I've heard more often when I've given this trip tip. I get it, OK? I admit, it does sound a little strange. Disneyland is in Florida, right? Sure, but hear me out: Tokyo Disneyland is the most visited park in the entire Disney empire, and well over ninety percent of the visitors are Japanese. So, this is a truly Japanese phenomenon, and the cultural traveler from the far West has a great opportunity at Tokyo Disneyland not only to see Mickey Mouse and ride a roller coaster, but also to take a trip right into the heart of the Japanese people's soul. So let's go!

Japan has, in recent years, become known for its so-called “kawaii culture”. Kawaii means cute and elements of kawaii culture are ubiquitous throughout the country. For example, in the form of drawn mascots for almost everything you might encounter, including cuddly plastic bears guarding construction sites or cute little tigers advertising for the Japanese army.

For most Japanese people, a visit to Disneyland is a celebration of kawaii and seems to be also behind the ever-popular Halloween. That's why this day in the park is usually spent dressed up. At least with mini mouse ears for the ladies and a Donald cap for the men, but also with full body costumes. Groups of young people, who elsewhere might be embarrassed to be seen anywhere near a Mickey Mouse, come to Tokyo with ten or twenty friends all dressed up in the same way. So it's not unusual to find yourself standing in a queue with a dozen or so cheerful Porky Pigs or being eyed with interest by a group of Winnie the Poohs.

On my first visit to Tokyo Disney, I took significantly more photos of the visitors around me than of any attraction in the entire park. And the many disguises are only one side of the experience. The other is the joy of experiencing the extreme environment of "theme park" with so many considerate and disciplined people. Queuing - pleasant everywhere, no one pushes, no one smells, no one is loud. Parades - everyone sits down dutifully and without being asked to do so on the asphalt along the parade routes, so as not to block the view of other guests further back. Unanswered questions - many park employees may not be able to answer due to lack of sufficient English, but an English-speaking supervisor is always activated in seconds and jumps right in. And, what I learned from American friends: The food at Tokyo Disney is worlds better than in the U.S., the park is also cleaner and better maintained, and supposedly Disney employees are nowhere friendlier in the world than in Tokyo. I can't judge the latter myself, but it sounds obvious.

Tokyo Disney is worth a visit because the park is virtually a model case of Japanese virtues. When observing the visitors who, thanks to their discipline and consideration, look after each other completely smoothly even in huge crowds and still have a lot of fun. And with the employees, whose self-image as hosts and will to perfection allows them to wave cheerfully to every child even after hours of service; when the anticipation of the end of the day is surely weighing on them, still they smile and wave.

4. Time travel from 1750 and several centuries of Japanese architectural history.

Edo Tokyo Open Air Architectural Museum, via Musashi-Koganei Station

About an hour outside Tokyo's inner wards is the Edo Tokyo Open Air Architectural Museum - one of the largest "hands-on" architectural museums in all of Japan. Unlike many other open-air museums, which often exist in Japan with a focus on a specific period or region, here buildings from many different eras have been gathered together.

Director Hayao Miyazaki visited this museum very often for inspiration while working on "Spirited Away" in the early 1990s - for many years the most successful Japanese animated film of all time.

The entrance fee of an absolutely unbeatable four bucks grants you access to a large park where you can spend several hours relaxing. Here you can find old farmhouses, large mansions with beautiful Japanese gardens, a wide variety of homes from across several centuries and even a large number of fully furnished stores from the past hundred years. While in Japan's capital there are almost only temples in terms of authentic historical buildings, here you can immerse yourself in a Tokyo that is almost impossible to find outside the museum gates due to the aftermath of earthquakes, fires, bombs and the ubiquitous modern wrecking balls.

A special highlight for me was that here you can visit a complete *sento*, an historic bathhouse. There are still some sentos in operation, but you can't normally take photos there, nor can you take a relaxed stroll through them. Here the museum offers a wonderfully visitor-friendly opportunity to stroll through this institution of Japanese bathing culture fully clothed and with a camera.

Equally impressive are some buildings from the 1960s that beautifully demonstrate how Japanese building traditions were skillfully mixed with Western influences. Incidentally, such buildings, with a mix of Japanese and Western architecture, were being built at the same time in California and all along the American West Coast. Cultural exchange was not a one-way street, and the celebrated bungalows of the American "Case Study House" program cite many Japanese design principles.

My personal favorites in the park, however, are the Meiji period villas. Built about a hundred years ago, they offer everything you dreamed of before visiting Japan: simple rooms of consummate beauty, magnificent sightlines, paper doors and wooden frames in artful simplicity, harmonious Japanese gardens in front of the houses and delicately scented tatami mats on the floors. It is hard to get more typical Japanese impressions without staying in a very good and expensive ryokan (a traditional hotel, see also the special chapter on this).

Incidentally, there is both a Western and a Japanese coffee and tea house in the park, both also in historic buildings. So you can even get a bowl of matcha or a large soft ice cream during a trip here. What more could you want?

Since I talked about Kawaii Culture in the previous chapter, I have to briefly talk about the mascot of this architecture museum. It is, drum roll ... a grinning caterpillar. Why it is. Of all Japan's disturbing or inappropriate mascots, this one was really a low point that I kind of remembered because of it. Aspiring readers who visit the museum after reading this book may please think of me when the giant caterpillar grins at them there.

5. Time travel to 1850 and vegetarian feast

Restaurant "Bon", via Iriya Station or cab. 1 chome-2-11 Ryusen, Taito City, Tokyo 110-0012

Getting to the restaurant "Bon" is unusually tedious. It is located in a sort of Bermuda triangle, equally difficult to reach from all relatively nearby subway lines. But the twenty-minute walk from Iriya Station, the first stop north of the massive Ueno Station on the Hibiya Line, is worth it. Bon is, perhaps also due to its location, a real "hidden gem". Here, in a restaurant that is over a hundred years old and very inconspicuous from the street, Buddhist temple cuisine is celebrated. Served as a series of courses, Bon features *shojin ryori*, a vegan cuisine here served in the style of the world-famous kaiseki cuisine.

For only about eight thousand yen, or seventy dollars, per person, you'll receive a friendly welcome after a successful reservation and you'll dive right behind the sliding door facing the street into another world. Once inside, you change from your shoes into the slippers provided and are led to one of the private dining rooms. Take a seat on the tatami floor, briefly take a gander at the room with its whitewashed walls, and the first dishes are served.

I will describe kaiseki cuisine in detail in the restaurant chapter, so for now I'll focus on Bon's exquisite shojin ryori multi-course meal. Put simply, you can expect beautifully arranged, highly seasonal, delicious vegetarian dishes in a seemingly never-ending sequence. All of this is presented in a calm and familiar manner that won't intimidate first-time visitors to Japan. This is known to happen in the more formal and more expensive kaiseki ryori restaurants.

If for whatever reason you don't travel far in Japan, don't have the time, money or nerve to stay at a traditional inn, a so called ryokan, and want to experience traditional Japanese hospitality, you should put a visit to this restaurant on your must do list. But don't forget to make reservations early. Even though there aren't too many tourists here the restaurant is very popular with Japanese patrons. It's gotten some fantastic reviews in vegetarian restaurant guides as well, which have recently started pulling foreigners all the way out here as well. But most of them come by cab anyway.

6. Time travel to 1950 and lively drinking

Via Shinjuku Sanchome Station

I include "Golden Gai" here, although it is mentioned in many city guides and is therefore not an insider tip. However, the popular descriptions are often imprecise and throw this very special neighborhood into the same corner as the surrounding district Kabukicho: beer and brothels, primitive and wild, like one wild bachelor party.

Golden Gai is one of the last original post-war pub districts in Tokyo, many of which were created after the Second World War in various parts of the city. Several very narrow alleys are home to over 250 impossibly tiny drinking establishments. Unfortunately, the way to this going-out experience leads through the not-so-nice corners of Tokyo, the aforementioned Kabukicho. Nightclubs, soaplands and "health" clubs can all be found here, guarded by unusually large and unusually grim-looking men in ill-fitting suits. This is also one of the very few areas in Japan where you actually hear about pickpockets. The gauntlet through the red-light district doesn't take long, and it's not terribly unsafe by international standards. After a few minutes, you reach Golden Gai, an overwhelming sea of flashing signs, narrow staircases, a cacophony of music, and the smell of beer and chicken skewers.

However, there is an "oasis entrance" to Golden Gai if you approach from Shinjuku Station. Cross Yasukuni Dori at the Picadilly Theaters to officially enter Kabukicho, and right across the street from the Shinjuku Ward Office you'll find a small opening at the street corner nestled between two commercial buildings. The "Four Seasons Pathway" is a narrow, paved green space that cuts walkers through the southern part of Kabukicho from Yasukuni Dori to a central intersection right in the middle of the neighborhood. The green space is fairly well-lit, and very quiet considering the raucous character of the surrounding district. On the eastern side is Golden Gai, and there are several entrances to get there directly from the Four Seasons Pathway. Much safer and prettier than approaching Golden Gai from Shinjuku Sanchome

Station to the east. *Editor's note:* As a former resident of Shinjuku who regrets ever leaving, I had to add this note about a very special entrance to Golden Gai.

Along the narrow alleys, two-story cottages are now lined up, most of which are no more than three meters wide. When you step through the door, you are right at the bar, with seating for maybe five but no more than ten. And that's all. On the upper floor, there is always a second bar on the same floor space, which, however, exists spatially, thematically, and usually also economically and operationally completely separate from the lower one.

Each of these bars is different, seeks its own special audience and usually reflects the taste or lack thereof of the owner or hostess down to the smallest detail. As a rule, the founder, owner and manager (all one person, mind you) stands behind the bar and looks after his guests seven days a week.

There are bars for everything and everyone. Death metal bars where you can't hear yourself think. Bon Jovi bars, where only the hits of that great New Jersey band are played, day in, day out (honestly, it's worse than torture). Eighties, seventies and sixties bars. Bars with a soccer theme and five TVs on five meter counters, all showing different games. Bars just for women, just for straight men, just for gay men and so on. It's hard to describe, but there is only one way to enjoy it: just open the door and see what awaits you inside.

On some doors it is clearly posted that foreigners are not welcome. This is very disturbing on a first visit. But such signs do not necessarily mean that the host is a Japanese Nazi, radical nationalist or xenophobe. It may simply be that bad experiences with a troop of drunken foreigners in combination with a lack of language skills on both sides have led to a once bitten twice shy stance by the proprietor. Or that the landlord can fill his mere five seats with regulars so well that he doesn't want to fill them with unintelligible bar hoppers. All this does not make such signs any better, but in Japan the fear of losing face or conflicts can be so great that creating clear conditions at the outset is preferable. As a visitor, you should simply accept this and move on.

I had my nicest evening at Golden Gai after one of the first Covid lockdowns, when the bars were just allowed to reopen, but there wasn't that much going on yet. Together with my German friend Carsten, who also lived in Tokyo for a few years, we strolled through the almost empty alleys in the evening and were able to calmly try to decipher door signs and bar names. After some time, we decided on a tiny bar on the top floor of a small house, above the window of which was actually written "German Music from the 80s". Upstairs we were greeted by an older Japanese barmaid, dressed more or less like Nina Hagen at her best (think "Karma Chameleon"-era Boy George sans hat, but as a raven-haired East German woman). With the neon-colored hair band, it was just incredible. The music was lively candy pop from the eighties, some embarrassing hits by Milli Vanilli and Modern Talking.

Quickly our hostess had recognized that we both spoke German - and we started an animated discussion with her about German pop music forty years ago, led with hands, feet and a lot of whistling and drumming bars on the table, And then, how could it be otherwise, she put on just for us Nena and the "99 Luftballons". We all sang together, united in German Japanese friendship.

There are comparable bars in many corners of Tokyo, but nowhere else did I find them as easy to find as here. At the same time, the whole neighborhood, with its dense but only two-story buildings, is very unusual in terms of urban planning. It is a living time capsule of a Tokyo - and who knows how long it will exist as it is now. There are repeated attempts to demolish the entire district. It would be possible to build fifty stories on this area, and fire protection, then hygiene regulations, and then earthquake prevention are cited whenever an attack is made on this urban artifact. You should hurry to visit here one evening before that is no longer possible.

If you find the area around Kabukicho too seedy or are worried that you won't be able to get into any pub in Golden Gai, you should look for guided tours there. There are quite loud pub crawl tours that only visit some of the few bigger locations in Golden

Gai, which thus fail to provide the experience you're actually here for. But with a bit of luck, you can find guides who go on tour with only three or four guests. This would make, for some very fun times, the perfect setting for a trip to Golden Gai.

City shopping for the advanced

Of course, you can go to thousands of great stores in Tokyo, without much background knowledge. But with the tips enclosed, I guarantee a nice broad spectrum of impressions, great opportunities for shopping - and various aha moments in which you can find descriptions from this book again.

1. Kappabashi Road

Via Tawaramachi Station

In many Asian cities, there are still streets and neighborhoods today where merchants and craftsmen of a very specific discipline have settled. You can still find this to a certain extent in Manhattan: The Garment District, the Diamond District, restaurant supplies on Bowery and so on.

In Tokyo, many streets that were once clearly defined in terms of their theme have been lined with a wide variety of stores in recent decades, so that you can usually buy a colorful mix of everyday necessities there. A nice exception, however, is the easily accessible Kappabashi Road. This street has been selling kitchen and cooking goods for decades over a span of about one kilometer. This street is thus perfect for finding nice souvenirs at fair prices.

Very fine and well-stocked specialty stores for Japanese kitchen knives can be found here, which are fully geared to tourists and whose staff can explain in fluent English all the peculiarities of any forging technique. And who, after you have chosen your knife, quite naturally fill out a sales tax refund form and explain to the happily surprised customer how to redeem it for cash at the airport.

Right next to the knife store, porcelain vessels in every conceivable pattern and shape are stacked up four meters tall, always packed in fives since four is an unlucky number in Japan.

As a rule, no one here speaks a word of English, but the sellers kindly fish every item off the wall that you would like to look at.

Another door down, there are all the stainless-steel tools you can admire every day while eating ramen. Small noodle strainers, large stirring spoons, noodle machines and ladles, plus hundreds of varieties of beautiful ramen bowls.

And in the next store they are obviously looking forward to tourists again, because they offer courses in model making. Why model making? Many of the dishes served at most restaurants in Japan are presented as wax or plastic models in the front display window or in a showcase. These deceptively realistic and appetizing models are made individually for each store on the basis of the dishes actually served there and are real eye-catchers. Here, in a workshop lasting several hours, you can now make your own plate of spaghetti Bolognese or a bowl of rice with vegetables and breaded schnitzel for eternity, with the same crispy, juicy hot look as the often-admired originals.

In short, Kappabashi is a great place if you want to bring back some valuable and at the same time useful things from Japan. It offers a nice balance of the old and established, sometimes a bit tarnished, but excellently sorted traditional stores - and for tourists optimized, but also very nice stores of shorter tenure.

2. Dentsdelion Antiques

Via Akihabara Station, 2-4-13 Taito City, Tokyo

Dentsdelion is a wonderful antique store within walking distance of the video game, arcade game, anime, manga, and high-tech paradise of Akihabara. The married owners, a Frenchman and a Japanese woman who share an encyclopedic knowledge about Japanese cultural and art history, welcome you personally to this small store. My first visit with them was more like a private tour of a historical museum than an afternoon of shopping. Yvan, the owner, knows about each of the thousands of items in his store, where it came from, what it was once used for, how it was made, and incorporates half the history of Japan in his explanations. For example, we moved from the pommel of a samurai sword to Asian blacksmithing in general, from there to Japanese bronze, talked briefly about Japanese incense ceremonies for which they use very nice bronze incense burners, and from there moved on to talk about the Buddhist deities of Japan. Which in turn led to us climbing the stairs to the upper floor and having various Buddha representations of the last five hundred years made of wood, bronze and stone explained to me.

If you have a real interest in historical Japanese art objects, then you should make your way to this beautiful store. Since the two owners, despite their great friendliness and zeal for work, are certainly not millionaires, it would of course be nice to buy something small after a long tour or visit.

3. BRING

Via Shibuya Station, 1-12-17 Shibuya, Tokyo

BRING is one of thousands of stores in Tokyo that sell secondhand goods. The focus in this store is on very rare, valuable streetwear. And that, in turn, has been a big scene in Tokyo for a good thirty years, longer than in many other parts of the world, which have only been overrun by the collab, limited edition and collectible wave in recent years.

At Bring, especially if you're into streetwear, you can touch things you've usually only seen in magazines or maybe on Instagram. Supreme x Louis Vuitton jackets at horrendous prices hang here just like rare Off-White Nikes.

What makes the store particularly worth visiting is a large selection of Japanese fashion brands. They all have their own flagship stores in Shibuya and Harajuku, to which you can of course make a pilgrimage. But in the basement of BRING, you can admire the highlights of recent years. Above all, streetwear by A Bathing Ape, Stüssy Japan or Hysteric Glamour, but also fashion by Issey Miyake, Comme des Garçons, Maison Kitsuné or Kenzo - although the latter two are strictly speaking French brands, which are nevertheless considered local heroes in Japan because of their Japanese designers.

However, contrary to what you might expect from the term "secondhand", the vast majority of products here are very expensive. Often, they cost many times the original price.

The store is more like a museum of contemporary art and pop art - where you can buy all the exhibits – If you can afford to.

4. Coffee Roast Vivace

Via Jiyugaoka Station, 3-6-22 Yakumo, Tokyo

This tiny coffee roastery is run by two generations of the Nakao family. Mom, dad and daughter offer one of the best selections of fresh, unroasted coffee beans in the whole city. You can choose your favorite variety from large bags and barrels, with exceptional, expert advice.

Then the beans are freshly roasted while you sit on the small terrace in front of the store and drink a freshly brewed coffee.

Each customer's order is roasted separately, so that an armada of gas-fired roasting drums constantly rotate noisily in the small store and slowly brown their contents. This creates the most intense coffee aroma I've ever had the pleasure of experiencing. The beans rumble everywhere, the gas flames hiss, and the whole store smells like a giant, slightly caked-on coffee bean.

The very sophisticated coffee culture of Japan is encapsulated in this store. And you can take home exceptional coffees in pretty packaging, both as gifts and for your own use.

In addition to freshly roasted coffee, there are also some pre-packaged roasts of the day to buy, as well as lots of coffee-making utensils. And, in small glasses with screw tops, daily freshly made tiramisu with a special house espresso. It is so beautifully chocolaty and bitter that the whole dessert, which is already very tasty, is catapulted to a new, even more excellent level.

The coffees to try are not made with a fancy portafilter machine. But filtered or prepared with small Bialetti pots on open gas flames. Taste-wise, all the variations I drank there are exceptionally good, and you really should enjoy a cup or two. In the warm season, it is best served as Iced Coffee, the favorite summer drink of the Japanese.

The small roastery is a bit off the beaten track in a very nice residential area. The best thing to do is to get yourself to Jiyugaoka Station, walk crisscross through some residential streets here and just have a look at some stores, houses and the hustle and bustle of affluent Jiyugaoka on the way - and then either stroll to the nearby

Komazawa Park, or make your way back to the city center from Toritsu-daigaku Station.

5. Don Quixote

Everywhere in Japan

Don Quijote, or simply "Donki" for short and colloquially, is a superstore chain with stores all over Japan. As a rule, all of the chain's stores are easy to spot from a distance, as they are adorned by huge signs in black, yellow and red - on which there is almost always a large blue penguin wearing a Santa hat.

For some reason, there is a rumor in many travel guides that donkis are bargain markets. This is not true, because the prices are clearly in the middle range. What donkis are, however, is very much how foreigners imagine oh-so-crazy Japan to be.

Donki assortment of products ranges from champagne and energy drinks in the basement to sex toys and stereo systems on the top floor. In between, there's pretty much everything Japan makes, or Japanese people might need.

Donkis are loud. Music plays everywhere, often different types of music at the same time. Mixed with the loud advertising messages from info screens and advertising announcements.

Donkis are colorful. Somehow everything is mixed up, there is a crazy abundance of objects that you never wanted to have, but that look appealing and scream "Take - me - with you! Next to cheap backpacks for five euros are designer bags for five hundred euros, and you don't really know what to look at in the chaos.

Donkis often seem trashy, not only because they are way too stuffed with merchandise, but also because the vast majority of the advertising posters in the store are hand-painted. Huge cardboard posters hang everywhere, advertising all kinds of products in large handwritten letters. On the cosmetics shelf, for example, there is a photo of a model with white skin next to a whitening cream, simply stuck to the shelf with adhesive tape. Next to it is a second piece of paper with a large speech bubble in which a text written in ballpoint pen explains the product and its benefits in detail.

Donkis, however, are a great place to shop despite the noise, chaos, and ramshackle atmosphere. For the simple reason that there is a lot here. For example, Western products that you might longingly miss. And lots of good Japanese products bundled in one place, especially food, cosmetics and alcohol of every kind and price range, for which otherwise you often have to go to different stores.

You can really stock up on everything to your heart's desire here. Very popular souvenirs are usually all products with Matcha, especially the green Kitkat bars with Matcha flavor. In contrast to the "sake-lime" and "salt plum" Kitkat variants tested in the brave self-experiment, these are also really very good.

In addition, there are many other Japanese sweets that look exotic and usually taste great. You can also buy sake and Japanese whiskey at Donki, the selection is very large, and the prices are fair. And I also loved buying birthday cards and the like there. With their beautiful Japanese motifs, they look refreshingly different from all the balloons, bears and cakes outside Japan - and you can take plenty of them home in your suitcase.

But since the stores are so chaotic, there are certainly many more great things there, but I just have not yet had the chance to discover them. I hope you have fun browsing and wish a few great discoveries in the personal Donki foray.

The country Japan

High-tech and plywood walls - Japanese houses

My first few weeks in my own Japanese home were marked by two things: confusion and incomprehension. Confusion because there are knobs and digital menus everywhere for things that should be available at the push of a button, like hot water. Incomprehension because I spent many hours in vain using Japanese instruction manuals, Google Translate, and internet videos trying to understand the basic mechanics of our home automation.

In hotels, you usually only experience a small part of the Japanese domestic technology universe, namely the fully automatic bidet toilets. And these already completely overwhelm the average visitor. You just want to press the one button for flushing, but you get lost between the intensity setting of the water jet, the heating control for the toilet seat, and the various scent and noise programs. Apply this cacophony of functions this to a whole house, and you can already imagine how it was for me.

After two weeks, I gave up and called our broker to help me. Embarrassed that he had rented an apartment to a client who did not understand what he had offered to them, but with great patience, he then explained all the buttons and knobs to me over several hours. And I labeled all the round, square and oval knobs with short German texts so that I wouldn't forget anything.

But what is so different about the Japanese house or apartment versus houses in Western countries? Almost everything. Let's start with the kitchen. In Japanese kitchens, there is usually no oven, which makes sense if you think about it. Can you think of any baked Japanese dish? I know I can't. At the same time, this explains to some extent the large number of bakeries everywhere. At a Christmas quiz in my office, there was once a question about who had ever baked a cake in their life. Only a quarter of the assembled colleagues had - and those were the ones who had once spent an exchange year in Europe or the USA.

However, instead of the oven there is another widely used appliance: a narrow pull-out grill under the stove tops. This is used diligently and with pleasure, especially to grill fish.

Dishwashers are quite common in Japan, but ours looked completely different from the one we had back home. Instead of having a flap to access the inside, it is designed as a pull-out drawer. You pull it out, pile the dirty dishes into it like a sink, and turn it on. Since the dishes are not neatly separated and stand in the water, the rinsing effect is rather poor with very high water consumption. This is also common knowledge, so the built-in dishwasher is often ignored, and dishes are washed by hand. Or, if space permits, the Japanese dishwasher drawer is replaced by a Western dishwasher. Incidentally, in Japan the German company Miele ranks high in the hierarchy of high-quality kitchen appliances. If you have money, you can wash and cook with Miele.

Just as I didn't understand at first how my Japanese colleagues could manage without an oven, they were equally shocked to learn that I didn't own a microwave. According to my non-scientific and not entirely representative analysis, the microwave is the one kitchen appliance that even the smallest one-room apartment in Japan cannot do without. One obvious advantage I learned: A microwave is really quite excellent for reheating rice. It becomes fluffy again and almost like fresh from the rice stove. In addition, this compact device is used above all to warm up the gigantic variety of ready-made meals from Japan's supermarkets. More details on this can be found in the konbini chapter.

Another feature of many Japanese kitchens, and this one you'll encounter in-room in many ryokans, is an electric kettle that boils three to five liters of water and then keeps it at or just under boiling temperature all day. With a quick push of a big orange button, the machine pumps the water into teacups, coffee mugs, or onto Cup Noodles. I loved this kettle because, for one thing, I had water at the perfect temperature for my green tea (eighty degrees) at all times. And for another, I had so much of this water conveniently available that I drank more, and I think healthier, throughout the day than I would have without it.

For us, the most obscure electrical device in the Japanese kitchen was quite small. A box measuring perhaps ten by ten centimeters with a display, a few LEDs and switches: the remote control for the bathtub. Really, a remote for the bath!

In many Japanese homes, you start the bath while you're in the kitchen. An identical control unit is on the wall in the bathroom, but for some reason it seems more natural to do this from the kitchen. My (slightly evil) suspicion is that this was set up so that the wife could continue cooking or doing the dishes when the master of the house asked for a bath. Unfortunately, I don't know the real reason, as no one could answer that question for me. But the fact is that these control units are present in many kitchens. Their functions include running the water, starting the heating in the bathroom, selecting the exact temperature of the bath water, and returning the water from the previous day to the desired temperature.

And here we are at the next special feature of Japanese living. That baths are very important here is probably common knowledge. But in a Japanese family, each members bathes each day. after taking a shower.

To understand the underlying logic: In the West, you bathe to get clean. In Japan, you bathe after you get clean. The bath is used for relaxation and a second, deep pore cleaning after the previous scrubbing off of dust and sweat in the shower. Soap is not added to the bath water, so remains nice and clean and can therefore be used without any problems by all family members one after the other, or even over several days, which is where the reheat function starts to make a lot of sense.

Unfortunately, the hot water supply only seems sophisticated in the bathtub. All other water connections run via primitive instantaneous water heaters. Central heating and the associated central hot water supply is rare in the Kanto region, where Tokyo is located. The instantaneous water heaters are usually located on the outside walls of apartments and houses, near the gas connection. The water-carrying pipes then usually run without insulation, bolted naked to the outside walls and exposed to wind and weather, to the taps of the house. This cheap construction not only looks shabby from the outside, it also causes various problems. In winter, the water in the pipes is very cold and takes forever to get warm. In summer, on the other hand, the pipes get so blazing hot from the sun that even turning on the cold water will burn you, which has actually happened to me! And, as expected, the pipes also like to burst when it gets cold enough.

Welcome to high-tech Japan.

Although it is quite cold throughout Japan from November to February and even bitterly cold in the mountainous regions, in the west along the Sea of Japan coast and to the north, central heating is very uncommon except for the northernmost island of Hokkaido. I always had the impression that Japanese somehow like to freeze. Or consider heat a reprehensible and effeminate invention of the West.

I got this impression especially when I saw how schoolchildren are sent to school or to the playground in the afternoon in December when temperatures are below zero. They like to go without a jacket, sometimes in a T-shirt, and surprisingly often in shorts. I couldn't figure this out. Maybe they were trying to toughen the kids up? Surely their parents couldn't be that ignorant?

But back to the Japanese house. Here there are several measures against cold, but each has its pitfalls.

Modern houses and apartments are usually heated with single-room air conditioners. This is fast, but it is energy inefficient, costly and produces extremely dry air. Any house that is heated with air conditioners also has a lot of humidifiers around. As you might have guessed, those also consume electricity.

Some very new houses have underfloor heating - de facto the only type of heating with pleasant radiant heat in Japan. As a rule, however, these heaters are also powered by electricity, which makes them expensive to operate. For inexplicable reasons, however, they are usually installed only in the living room, even in new buildings. Hallways, bathrooms and bedrooms are cold next to them.

Probably the most common heater in Japan is actually the kerosene burner. And because Japan loves to perfect proven techniques rather than discard them, there is a huge selection of computer-controlled kerosene burners with electric blowers, automatic ignition and sophisticated anti-petroleum odor mechanisms. You place these stoves in various kilowatt strengths in the room you want to heat, order a 20-liter can of kerosene, fill up your stove, and then let the warm air blow around your ears. This works quite well, but has often been the reason for burning down entire streets. In addition, such a stove with its open flame destroys plenty of oxygen, so that after one or two hours of cozy heating you slowly doze off ...

That's why to this day there is probably the most traditional route to Japanese coziness in the winter months: the kotatsu. Not to be confused with tonkatsu, which is a breaded pork cutlet. I used to mix up the two words, making for various very funny or very embarrassing moments in Japan, depending on your perspective.

The kotatsu is a low table with a fixed, cozy blanket all around and an electric heating module under the tabletop, which in the past was a coal basin. When you gather with your family at the kotatsu, all your legs tucked under the warm table, the heavy cozy blanket falling over your hips, and dinner or something to nibble on the table, it really is a very nice, homely way to spend some time. A Japanese friend once told me that nothing reminds her so much of her childhood as sitting at a kotatsu and nibbling freshly peeled tangerines.

The classic and consistent handling of cold in Japan looks like this: When you get up from the heated kotatsu at some point, you walk through the ice-cold room to take a bath, which has been preheated by the button from the kitchen. There you warm up again for half an hour in hot water. And from there you go straight to your bed or futon, making sure not to grow cold before snuggling up under one or two thick blankets.

With the sewing machine over four-story highways

Tokyo by car is hell. Not on the main roads. There are traffic jams there, but this is true of every big city. No, Tokyo's problem is that it is characterized by countless narrow, winding and confusing side streets and alleys that are made for bicycles or maybe for rickshaws, but definitely not for cars.

I never expected that such a supposedly ultra-modern city would consist mostly of narrow streets that you might expect in Rome. In contrast to Rome, however, in Tokyo there are also huge electricity poles made of sturdy reinforced concrete on every street. Almost every one of these thousands of posts bears clearly visible traces of car paint, testimony to many generations of city cars whose drivers tried to squeeze too close to one of the poles. The only way to get through these alleys by car reasonably unscathed is by kei car.

In Japan, there are two categories of cars: conventional passenger cars like those used in various colors, shapes and comfort classes like in Europe and the US - and kei cars. A kei car must adhere to very strict rules regarding its compact dimensions and limited engine power. Narrower than a Mini Cooper, no more than 11ft long and no more than 64 horsepower.

Naysayers claim that a kei car has more in common with a shoebox on wheels, powered by a sewing machine, than with a car. But that doesn't do justice to these microcars, which account for around forty percent of all passenger cars sold in Japan.

Current kei-car models cost about fifteen to twenty thousand dollars. In return, they have super-practical sliding doors, an unexpectedly large amount of interior space and plenty of electronic gadgets ranging from a 360-degree exterior camera to a DVD player. What's more, kei cars are exceptionally agile. No matter how absurdly sharp a curve, how narrow the phalanx of electricity poles, how many Japanese mothers are coming toward you with their bicycles on both sides of the road; the kei car fits through. In Tokyo, I loved jetting through the city in our little white Mitsubishi EK-X. I was really able to get around in it. It felt like sewing, because as I said, the engine really does sound like a sewing machine running significantly too fast. Hopefully, EVs will remedy this in the near future.

If you are traveling by car outside the big cities, however, it is better to leave your kei car at home. Many Japanese rent a larger car, preferably a spacious van. And off they go on the excellently developed highways. Driving on Japanese highways is an experience in itself. Unfortunately, the speed is often limited to barely 50mph, and at 75mph, even on Japan's smooth-as-glass roads, it's over. So, your cruising speed always remains consistently low, but that makes it easier to enjoy the ride, and that is certainly worth it!

In Japan, there are gigantic road structures that even non-engineers can only admire. Interchanges of three highways, built entirely in the form of bridges, on five different levels above the ground. Tunnel entrances, where the highway first spirals five rounds of three hundred and sixty degrees into the ground before continuing deep under the city. Highways through Tokyo or the port of Nagoya, for example, that really are "high" because the roads constantly run for many miles at the level of the tenth floor of all adjacent buildings. Anyone who has ever played car racing on a Playstation will immediately remember game scenes.

The most frightening structure we drove through was a tunnel exit. We drove a few miles through a mountain on its flank, but the tunnel didn't exit into a valley as usual, but instead right out of a sheer rock face about a hundred meters above the valley. From there, we were led down a long, winding elevated roadway, hardly confidence inspiring, and somewhere along this route there was a rocky ledge on which the road then continued towards the valley. So, we spiraled down meter by meter, in seemingly endless circles. The problem for me (and my stomach) was that this steel serpentine construction was almost free-floating on the mountain. As you spiraled down, you saw nothing deep below you for a long time, and then finally a river. I prayed all the way down until we had solid asphalt under our wheels again.

On the other hand, many of the rest areas in Japan are just fantastic. Perfectly clean, spacious, with various typical Japanese fast-food restaurants (ramen, rice dishes, tonkatsu and curry) and very often a konbini with the standard Japanese prices (no price gouging of tourists here!). And the restrooms at all the rest stops are really wonderful. Public toilets are plentiful in Japan anyway and often very well maintained, but the freeway toilets are real celebrations of Japanese toilet culture.

This starts with the fact that there are always some completely covered parking spaces for people with disabilities directly in front of the restrooms. When it comes to the toilets themselves, visitors can choose exactly what they need. How about a standard toilet with eight water programs for cleaning your bottom or an additional music button that plays loud water sounds from loudspeakers so that you don't disturb other people with your dynamic bowel sounds? Or a cubicle with a child seat on the wall so that one's offspring are secured while mom or dad relieve themselves next to them? Maybe the cabin with a raised floor space where you can change without having your socks touch the dirty floor? Perhaps today we go for the children's cabin, which offers not only a mini toilet, but also a shrunken urinal for the male offspring, a small play corner (if you have to handle two children in succession), a changing table with diaper pail and of course a children's sink next to the adult sink - with extra fragrant children's strawberry soap.

The parking lots, like the restrooms, are free of charge, which is not a matter of course in a country where parking a car is often a challenge and very often expensive. If you pull off the highway and explore local Japanese roads, you will come upon the ubiquitous managed parking facilities. The market leader in parking facilities in Japan is "Times Parking", whose yellow and black signs accompany you throughout Japan. Times and many other providers have large parking areas and parking garages available, but the vast majority of these spaces are only intended for about one to five cars.

In tight cities like Tokyo, private citizens often lease the one or two parking spaces in front of their house to Times, whereupon the company sets up a pay parking lot there. The same happens on conveniently located plots of land a few months before they are to be built on. Times quickly covers the ground with blacktop, affixes signs, and then rents them out by the hour. These short-term parking spaces are usually equipped with steel immobilizers. When you park your car in a free space, a steel folds up under the car to stop it from rolling out. Only when you pay does it fold down again and the car can drive.

In our neighborhood, such a parking lot was once installed after the demolition of a house. Within a single week, a brown clay surface was transformed into a complete parking lot with ten electronically monitored parking spaces, neon signs, vending machines and ATMs.

These parking lots can also be used for a lesson on consumer protection in Japan, which is very bad, in many respects. In the case of parking lots, it expresses itself in the pricing. If common accounts are to be believed, years ago there was often very aggressive abuse of parking lots with extortionary prices by the Yakuza. Hundreds of dollars were demanded from people who had parked their cars for only a few hours - but according to legend, several well-built and bad-tempered men always presented the parkers with a small sign that actually stated that the hour here cost the equivalent of a hundred dollars. To prevent this, it was decided that the price of each parking space must be displayed very large - accordingly, the price signs at parking spaces are now always several meters wide. However, there is no regulation as to which price must be indicated, how large and with what frequency.

So have some fun and study these ubiquitous signs in the cities. Since they contain almost only numbers, you can understand them quite well even without knowledge of Japanese. Pricing structures vary widely per lot. Sometimes you're charged in 60-minute increments, sometimes 8 minutes, sometimes 25 minutes. And the prices per increment change based on day of the week and time of day. The week's lowest rates, like Sunday night to Monday morning, are displayed most prominently, and these are a fraction of the rates charged most other times.

At any rate, one gets the impression that Japanese parking lot operators are very well connected with the government. Otherwise, I can hardly explain why they are allowed to offer such completely non-transparent prices even after a supposedly customer-friendly tightening of the law.

Suitcase ban on the fastest train in the world

Why were there four tickets in the envelope? My colleague Mika had gotten them for my trip from Tokyo to Nagoya and back. I found it strange that there were four tickets for only one passenger (me). My long-awaited ride on the Shinkansen turned out to be strange all around.

I wanted to buy the tickets online, but that didn't work. Mika said she would be happy to do it for me as she had to go to the station anyway. So, I told her she could just send the tickets to my cell phone. There was a lot of confusion as to what I meant by that, and I then learned that online tickets for the Shinkansen are not an option for those who are not fluent in Japanese. Self-printed QR code tickets simply do not exist. You can't buy tickets online in English, nor can you get anything digital after paying cash. There is a very nice Suica Mobile app available that allows you to buy tickets on your phone, but this app is not only available only in Japanese, but only in the Japanese app store, requiring you to change the country of your app store before you can even find it in a search! The only way to get on one of the world's most modern express trains as a foreign traveler or resident foreigner who is not fluent in Japanese is through a ticket vending machine that ejects small pieces of printed paper. And lots of them.

One of the tickets for the base fare between the two stations, and the other is for the Shinkansen surcharge. The same applies for the return trip. So if you're traveling with a family of four, you'll have sixteen small tickets to look after. And don't you dare lose one: You need the tickets just to enter the platform, and then again to leave it. We once misplaced one of my son’s tickets, only realizing at the exit gate. I stood around completely stressed and sweating for ten minutes in front of the exit gate, in order to look for the missing ticket in my son’s bags, my bags and finally all of our hand luggage. Fortunately, it eventually reappeared crumpled and somewhat sticky in a children's book - and we were able to leave the platform without penalty.

Once you get used to the ticket madness, though, traveling by Shinkansen is a great thing. Unless you get lost, you simply walk from the subway to your Shinkansen platform. Some stations have different Shinkansen lines, which in turn belong to different operators. Therefore, it is important to be sure to look for the correct color or symbol of the line you need. Beyond that, not much can go wrong.

The long-distance trains themselves generally run at a frequency that would do credit to any of Europe's inter-city trains. Trains depart every three to five minutes, depending on the destination and time of day. The good thing is that you always get a train. The bad thing is that if you have a reservation, it is only valid for the train you have booked. Otherwise, you have to choose your seat or stand for two hours at one hundred ninety miles per hour. On most of the Shinkansen lines, however, there are some fixed carriages that are completely unreserved, and accordingly you should queue there if you don't have a reservation for reasons of time or economy. These special carriages are always well marked and can usually be asked about in English.

There is no such thing as a reversed car order in Japan. Car seventeen is always where car seventeen is on the track. And the doors of car seventeen will open exactly to the centimeter where they are marked on the platform. Shinkansen drivers are probably the only people who do their job more diligently than Japanese metro drivers.

Before I get on a Shinkansen, I always buy a bento box on the platform. Bentos are the greatest addition to train travel since the invention of the rolling suitcase. Which you don't need at all in Japan, of all places, but we'll get to that later.

Bentos are, simply put, food boxes. Usually with rice to fill you up. And all possible or impossible supplements. Often very, very beautifully arranged, versatile with fish, meat and various vegetables and salads and sauces and simply delicious. I've never had a bad bento. There are children's bentos, spicy bentos, mild bentos, bentos with just eel or grilled meat or especially for vegetarians: just about any need is fulfilled by bentos. And nowhere are there as many bentos as at large train stations. The standard price is around ten dollars and for that you get a freshness and variety that makes any McDonald's menu look very old and very unhealthy. The important difference here is that you eat your bento cold, but, really, which McDonald's meal is still warm once you've carried it all the way to the train?

As I mentioned before, you don't need rolling suitcases in Japan, especially not on the Shinkansen. You might even be punished for using them as there is only room for four large wheeled suitcases in each carriage. You have to reserve these seats in advance, otherwise you'll be in trouble with the conductor. But how do you, then, get your luggage from A to B? With the Takkyubin. Takkyu...what?

Takkyubin is an extremely well-developed parcel delivery service in Japan, offered by various companies like Sagawa Express and Yamato. To use Takkyubin, you simply go to the nearest Konbini, to your hotel concierge, or go to Yamato's English-language website. With Takkyubin, you can ship just about anything within Japan. In fishing ports, a Takkyubin counter is often located right next to the fish market, so tourists and restaurant owners can have their purchases sent home express and frozen. I once received a whole pallet of delicious white peaches from friends via Takkyubin, who had discovered them the day before on a plantation near Mount Fuji and had them sent to us in Tokyo.

But for me the simplest and most practical use case for Takkyubin is for suitcases and sports luggage. In winter, thousands of Tokyo residents take the Shinkansen for a weekend of skiing. After a two-hour ride from the capital, they arrive at the ski slopes of Nagano. But on these trains to the snow, you won't see a single pair of skis. No one is knocked down on the platform by two-meter-long Atomic ski packages. Instead, all skis travel in parallel to their owners via Takkyubin, are delivered there shortly before their arrival at the hotels, and then either brought to the room or kept ready in special storage rooms behind the reception desk. There, the travelers arrive relaxed and with light luggage, grab their ski gear, change briefly and are already on the slopes three hours after departure from Tokyo.

In very many guides about Japan, the Japan Rail Pass is advertised for the use of the Shinkansen network, with which only tourists residing outside Japan can use the trains for several days at a fixed price. However, the price of this pass is quite high, despite the discount. Therefore, it should be mentioned here that ANA also offers a "Discover Japan Fare" for non-Japanese for domestic flights, which is close in price to the Rail Pass, but much more flexible. That's why I wouldn't miss out on a Shinkansen trip, the most obvious is always the Tokyo - Kyoto route, but you can also book this separately and fly to other destinations in the island kingdom according to personal preference. Takkyubin of course also works for air travel, so you can travel comfortably with hand luggage in both modes of transport.

Frogs, bamboo and dreariness - Japanese countryside party

After a few weeks of driving around Tokyo and feeling increasingly confident in Japanese traffic, I thought narrow roads and convoluted routing could no longer shock me. So we took off for our first land trip, a trip to Mount Takao. That was a mistake.

A friend had told me that it was best to take the train to this popular mountain excursion near Tokyo because of the limited parking availability. In good German style, I thought, nonsense, if parking is really full, I'll just park on a nearby dirt road into the forest and we'll hike a little further. This, however, turned out to be a grave miscalculation. By 11:00am all parking lots were already occupied and there are dirt roads in Japan. They simply do not exist. We drove around the place twice from back to front, but no chance to get rid of our car anywhere. That after an hour and a half drive and great anticipation of a spring hike.

To save the situation, I decided to follow a country road on good luck. Somewhere there would be, hopefully, a parking lot for hikers? To make it short: no, there wasn't. Even in the countryside, the rule is that either someone has set up a paid parking lot or an organizer provides parking. Otherwise, there is simply no chance to get rid of your vehicle. On top of that, looking for a parking space on the off chance can get you into situations in the countryside that even make a supposedly hard-boiled Tokyoite like me exhausted.

The greatest evil here are roadside water channels. These are generally either rain gutters, or irrigation canals for farmland. They are everywhere. Next to rice fields, next to gardens, next to houses, all the way up mountain roads. Up to one meter deep, about half a meter wide - and never equipped with a railing or even a guardrail. If you drive too far along the edge, you tip half your car into it. Combined with roads that spontaneously narrow to just two meters wide after a mile of relaxed straight driving, and curve radii that even a bicycle can barely manage, these ditches produce as many stress hormones as a roller coaster ride without safety bars. It's terrifying. To top it all off, the ditches are favorite stomping grounds for snakes during the rainy season. So even if you walk along these canals on a village road without a car, they still scare you because of their crawling and screeching creatures within.

The gutters in the countryside exist mainly to grow rice. On Honshu, Japan's main island, rice is always grown wet - that means on completely flooded fields. Such fields with fresh rice grasses look very beautiful and they shine in a very intense, fresh green. And besides bamboo forests, rice fields in sight have always given me the nice feeling of being in a really exotic place far from home.

However, rice paddies also have a downside if you live near them in the summer. For one thing, lots of insects thrive on the standing water, especially mosquitoes. All day long, but especially at sunset - the only way to protect yourself from being eaten is with harsh DEET chemicals or a very smoky campfire.

On the other hand, millions of frogs live in the rice paddies, where they pose a very special challenge for the rest-seeking city dweller. The hopping amphibians are unimaginably loud. The croaking is very beautiful and atmospheric at a distance of a few hundred meters. But when your hotel or vacation home borders directly on a rice field, early sleep is out of the question. The croaking frogs develop a volume that makes every highway seem like a monastery of silence in comparison, and these cute animals constantly animate each other to join in properly. If one frog starts croaking, seconds later hundreds of frogs are croaking together. It is not until late summer, long after the frog mating season, that the Japanese countryside quiets down again.

Besides the wonders of nature, Japan is unfortunately often not very exciting outside of big cities or special historical and religious sites. Villages and small towns often look a bit run down. This is due to the juxtaposition of rusting bridges, more or less unkempt houses and small stores that were last renovated when Michael Jackson and Whitney Houston still had number one hits in Japan. In somewhat larger cities, there are new stores, but then almost without exception as part of a shopping mall on the outskirts of town. Here, huge supermarkets, pachinko halls, fast-food restaurants and car dealerships line up next to each other. It always reminded me a lot of scenes from American soap operas, only instead of pickups in the large parking lots, there are a fleet of Kei Cars and Toyota Prius hybrids.

Therefore, I would also advise against planning a supposedly romantic road trip through Japan. Unfortunately, most of the country is not as magical as in many anime. It makes more sense to pick out different highlights you'd like to visit and then combine that with a side trip to a more remote area somewhere during your trip. There are so many great temples, natural spectacles or other sights spread all over the country that you can easily take a look at the villages around. This gives you a more complete picture of Japan, although unfortunately this often means rather disappointing insights into a rather dull world of life. From which most young Japanese want to escape as quickly as possible - one of the many reasons why Tokyo and the other major Japanese cities are constantly growing, while entire villages are abandoned and left to decay.

Tank barriers in paradise - Japanese beaches and bays

The US has a coastline, all islands included, of about 12,500 miles. Comparably small Japan, on the other hand, has a 19,000 miles. Fifth place in the world, even ahead of Australia. However, this seemingly endless coastline is perceived by most Japanese as more of a threat than anything else. Storm surges, typhoons, tsunami waves and foreigners – many threats have come or at least historically came from the sea. Accordingly, large parts of this coastline present themselves as well protected. Romantic sandy beaches with palm trees are almost always absent. Instead, unimaginable quantities of armored barriers pile up on the edge of the Pacific. The technical term for these huge reinforced concrete elements: tetrapods. Each one weighs about six tons and is designed to break the force of the oncoming water. Tetrapods belong to Japan like sushi and sake. Unfortunately, they are not as beautiful to look at. On many stretches of beach that are open for swimming, you can see tetrapods fifty meters ahead in the water. Or they pile up to the right and left of the beach, where in other countries you would rather expect a pretty grassy dike.

When tetrapods are not in use, the Japanese coast is often fortified directly with walls. Or it consists of a harbor area. Or a steep coast. In any case, it is really rare to find a natural beach. But of course there are bathing beaches. Often a bit shorter than expected and often framed by industrial plants on both sides. But they do exist, and in the hot Japanese summer they are the perfect waterfront refuge.

Although summer is very hot, as mentioned, and it would definitely be warm enough to swim from May to September, the official swimming season in Japan lasts only four weeks. It starts in mid-July and ends on August 16. During these four weeks, the beaches turn into big public festivals. Restaurants are set up, additional showers and toilets are installed, a lifeguard stands every twenty-five meters, and surfing is temporarily banned in large sections in favor of playing children and swimming summer visitors. Day after day, Japanese now flock to the beach to enjoy a nice day out with friends or family. The emphasis here is on "one". As a rule, most people only make the effort to go on such a beach excursion once a year. But then also properly. With tents, parasols, folding chairs and tables, barbecues and even fireworks. Such a beach day is a real family celebration, comparable with the picnics at the cherry blossoms, only on the beach and in swimsuits.

Before and after the bathing season, the beaches are also open, but they are much quieter then. Surfers usually dominate the scene now, and families with small children play in the sand or surf. Surfing is a real popular sport in Japan, along with baseball and golf. Used surfboards and wetsuits can be bought by the hundreds in the large second-hand stores, and surfboards on the roofs of kei cars or on the side of bicycles are a very typical sight on Japan's coasts.

Remarkably, Japanese public beaches never charge admission. Often you can get to the sea quite well by public transport, from Tokyo this is even the standard. If you do arrive by car, however, you have to be very early to secure a paid parking space. On the beach itself, it is absolutely fine and in high summer there is no alternative to setting up a parasol or beach shell as sun protection. However, what is not okay at all are visible tattoos. They are forbidden on almost all Japanese beaches, as well as in onsens, or hot spring baths. The vast majority of Japanese bathers are not further affected by this, as there are very few tattoo wearers in Japan. However, if someone has had a tattoo permanently embellished, it is usually enough to cover it with some textile on the beach and that's it. Even if a huge tattooed work of art shimmers through fabric, as is so often the case in Japan, everyone is satisfied if the official rule of not showing off has obviously been respected, regardless of what can be guessed under the thin textile.

However, a real problem of bathing in Japan are the dangers in the water. Basically, there are more dangerous animals in Japan than is commonly thought. In the water, this applies above all to dangerous jellyfish, poisonous or spiny fish and, in the south, additionally to poisonous sea snakes, poisonous starfish and poisonous sea urchins. Hotel beaches, for example on Okinawa, are therefore often secured with close-meshed nets against uninvited sea dwellers. These hotel beaches do cost an entrance fee, but to me personally it's worth it. On one of our first days on vacation in Okinawa, I was snorkeling in a coral reef despite some warnings about poisonous sea snakes, when a long coiled creature swam by within sight of me. Maybe it was just a lone eel. But I've never crawled ashore as fast as I did at that moment in my entire life. And since I'd rather worry about the next cocktail than my life on vacation, we were never in the water again in Okinawa on beaches with free access and no safety nets.

Everything so Murakami here - Japanese forests

Robots, fast trains, strange automata. That's what many who haven't been associate with Japan. Not very many come up with "forested." Yet Japan has nearly as much forest area as Montana, Georgia and Colorado combined.

In Japan, the forest is a wilderness. A wild, dense, green mélange of trees, bushes, bamboo, bears and snakes. It is difficult to impossible to move in the Japanese forest on good luck. For the most part, it is simply an impassable, impenetrable jungle.

The relationship of the Japanese to the forest is complex. Basically, traditional Japanese culture views nature as being inhabited by a large number of spirits or kami. These kami are worshipped, be it with simple garlands made of rice straw and paper, or with huge temple complexes. A particularly large tree, a mountain peak or just a beautiful stone may be considered sacred. There are probably more spirits per hectare of forest in Japan than there are squirrels in New England. Much esteem is also given to particularly beautiful or imposing parts of the forest.

At the same time, people fear the forest for its darkness and all the creatures it harbors. There is hardly a hiking trail in Japan that does not warn of killer hornets, bears, or both.

A great example of the multi-layered significance of the forest in Japan can be found in various books by Haruki Murakami. Currently Japan's most widely read author, Murakami often lets his protagonists experience supernatural and eerie things in the forest. Contemplation and reflection on the one hand. On the other hand, apparitions of mythical creatures, ghosts and dwarves and encounters with time-traveling people.

If you like Murakami, you have to spend a day or two in the Japanese forest. This opens up a whole new approach to his books and makes many of the "crazy" things in his stories suddenly seem a little more credible. At least one understands how the Japanese forest could have such a lasting impression on him.

If you are only traveling in Tokyo but want to get a small impression of the Japanese wilderness, you should visit the "Todoroki Ravine Park" for a couple of hours. The description can be found in the chapter "The hidden wonders of the capital".

If you want to dive into the Japanese forest a little more intensively, you can do so, for example, in the Aokighara Forest, close to Mt. Fuji and only about two hours' drive from Tokyo. This forest is so beautiful, dark and mystical that it is called "The Sea of Trees" in Japanese. However, it also gained sad notoriety as the "Suicide Forest." Up to two hundred and fifty people take their own lives here every year among roots, giant trees and mossy boulders.

Much less dramatic is a visit to a forest park. These are large parks around metropolitan areas where the stressed urban population can experience the forest in a very safe and family-friendly way. Each of these parks is designed a little differently, of course, but basically you can expect several miles of nicely laid out hiking trails, very good signage, numerous lookout points, landscaped picnic areas, well-maintained restroom facilities, and well-cooled or, in winter, heated vending machines. Some parks also offer small museums, traditional activities such as indigo dyeing or pottery, and provide large barbecue areas.

Reservations are usually required for these barbecue areas, but if this is taken care of by Japanese friends or the hotel concierge, you can spend a very nice afternoon in the countryside here. And since convenience is very important in Japan, you don't have to bring anything to the barbecue. The range of meats is ordered in advance, the barbecue fire is lit by the expert who is always present, and a brand-new and still sealed barbecue grill is also already included in the carefree package booked.

Of brown bears, killer hornets and sea snakes - Japan's dangerous wildlife

My first encounter with Japanese fauna, which surprised me, was many years ago in Kyoto. We had visited a very beautiful temple and slowly wound our way up a mountainside between its building sections. Once at the top, we enjoyed the view of the grounds and simply followed a path that got lost in the trees ahead of us. Somehow, we thought, it would surely lead us to another temple, or to a cemetery, or to something else worth seeing.

After a few hundred meters, our path tapered off into a trail, and a few minutes later it simply melted into the leaf-covered forest floor. In the heat of that summer afternoon, the forest was beautiful. Very dense, but the foliage shimmered intensely in a wide variety of greens. For me, these many shades of green make up the greatest magic of the Japanese forest; everywhere in the country, forests appear deeper, more vivid, more charming than in many other parts of the world. At the same time, the many tall trees provided us with pleasant shade, and accordingly, in good spirits, we trudged on without a visible path. I walked a few meters ahead of my wife and was telling some story when I casually kicked aside a branch in the foliage. While lunging with my foot, however, the branch moved - I stopped so abruptly that I almost tripped over my own feet. A huge snake was moving in the foliage.

Now, of course, one can discuss what "huge" means. For me, who until then had seen at most a grass snake dozing in the sun, it was at first a gigantic snake. Somewhere between boa and cobra. It was quite brown in color, which is why I had mistaken it for a branch. I couldn't estimate its length exactly, but it was certainly over two meters.

And so there I was, in the forest above Kyoto, with my wife behind me and the biggest snake of my life so far practically next to my foot. Fortunately, the snake felt the same as me. Obviously very frightened by this huge, very pale man with the wide-open eyes, it quickly took to its heels and meandered at impressive speed into the undergrowth.

Back at our hotel, I learned that the snake was probably a Japanese rat snake. Up to seven feet long, brownish, likes to travel in the forest and non-poisonous. But that was not written on its shiny scales when I discovered it next to me. However, our landlady said she never goes through leafy forest areas without a stick. That was quite reckless - whether we had not seen that all the paths near the temple had been carefully swept? Yes, of course we had seen that but we only thought of ubiquitous Japanese cleanliness, not of snake prevention.

To perfect the snake picture: Of course, there are also poisonous snakes in the Japanese forest. For example, the brown-red mamushi, which, however, only grows to about half a meter. Much more venomous than the small mamushi are its sisters, the Okinawa habu (which, according to reports, also likes to haunt houses in Okinawa), the tiger snake (which, to the delight of all farmers, lives mainly in rice fields) and finally the extremely venomous half-banded flat-tail - a sea snake with a preference for coral reefs around the tropical islands in southern Japan.

Another challenge in the Japanese forest is bears. On the main island of Honshu, where Tokyo and Kyoto are also located, there are some 10,000 Japanese black bears according to official estimates. These cute animals weigh around a hundred kilograms, grow up to five feet are unfortunately very short-sighted. The latter leads to the fact that they notice hikers sometimes very late and then bite when startled. To prevent this, one always goes hiking near black bears with a small bear bell on their backpack. The ears of the Ursus Japonicus are very good, and as a rule the animals take to their heels as soon as they hear a bell ringing in the distance. Despite these precautions, incidents with black bears occur from time to time, which can also be fatal. Accordingly, we were always very careful and rang like a whole herd of cows when we were hiking on Honshu.

Even more dangerous than black bears are brown bears, which in Japan approach the size of polar bears and weigh around five hundred kilograms. They live exclusively in the far north, on Hokkaido. With the sometimes aggressive representatives of this species, a bell doesn't do too much good. Instead, it is recommended to carry large bottles of bear spray. Therefore, we always had the officially recommended "Police Magnum Pepper Spray for Bears and Bad Persons" on our belt holster during our hikes on Hokkaido. Fortunately, we didn't have to try it out to see if it would have worked. But after the sad record number of twelve people were killed by brown bears on Hokkaido in 2021, we felt much safer with the spray.

While there are almost never warning signs for snakes, although they meander through city parks even in the middle of Tokyo, one is warned of bears again and again with yellow signs. On forest paths, campsites or parking lots there are clear pictures with a bear, many exclamation marks and sometimes a skull and crossbones.

Even more common than these warnings about the really big animals are signs warning about insects, specifically the Asian giant hornet. In recent years, isolated specimens of this species have appeared in the USA, where they are aptly named "Murder Hornet". However, they have earned this title because of their attacks on bee colonies, not on humans.

My first and fortunately so far only encounter with the giant hornets left quite an impression. My wife and I were on mountain bikes on Hokkaido, near the former Olympic city of Sapporo. It was very warm, I wore a yellow shirt and pedaled neatly sweaty up a mountain. At some point on the side of the road, I noticed that I kept crunching over very large, dead hornets. The reason for this, I later learned, is the rather slow flying speed of these almost palm-sized insects. They are so slow that they are constantly being hit by cars near roads, leaving their lives on grilles and windshields. However, because they are large and robust, they do not simply burst, but lie well preserved on the road afterwards. The sight of all these dead and really very large monsters was quite, let's say, "special." It became really unpleasant when I heard a very distinct humming noise on my bike. First on my right, then again on my left, then again on my right - I was being circled by a huge hornet.

Now you have to know that I am already afraid of the common wasp found in Europe or the US. It may be silly, but I can't help myself with wasps, I go into a mild panic, usually jumping up and unable to eat or drink anything until the unwelcome visitor has disappeared again or been swatted. And so now, in the middle of a mountain in Hokkaido, the biggest hornet ever, circling around me like a bird of prey, while I'm riding a bicycle. When I slowed down, I noticed the buzzing got louder, so I stepped on the gas. We had already cycled about 50 miles, in a good hour we wanted to be at our destination, my legs were tired, and I was thirsty. But on this mountain, beset by a giant insect, I was in the form of my life. I pedaled up the mountain at a constant 12 mph, the absolute maximum speed I could manage. For several miles always accompanied by the hornet and in real panic that this huge critter wanted to sting me. After what felt like an eternity, just before the pass to be crossed and many meters higher up than at the beginning of the buzzing escort, the hornet disappeared. I pedaled on in panic until I reached the pass, listened, slowed down, listened again, and it was really gone. I plopped down next to my bike and just lay there for the next quarter of an hour.

A short while later, we were finally at the hotel, and after check-in and a wonderfully relaxing cleanse in the onsen, I read who or what had accompanied me there today, and why. According to this, the species of Asian Giant Hornet is not aggressive per se, but it is sensitive to bright colors and strong smells. So in my sweaty yellow jersey I certainly wasn't deescalating things. If you are stung, the sting with the approximately two-inch-long stinger is described as "exceptionally painful." Up to forty people in Japan die each year as a result of hornet stings, as the strong venom causes allergic reactions more quickly than those of other wasps or bees. This makes the hornet, though smaller, much more lethal on aggregate than snakes or bears. Hallelujah... Fortunately I had pedaled so furiously during the ascent that I was spared an even closer acquaintance. But since this adventure, Japanese hornet warning signs are a clear sign for me to turn right back around.

The mother of all natural disasters: Earthquake

My first earthquake occurred about eight weeks after we moved to Tokyo, around two o'clock at night. I have rarely been as frightened as I was that night. I almost didn't feel the quake - but four smartphones in the house, two of them next to our bed, suddenly sounded the alarm at full volume. I didn't know what was happening to me at all. Half asleep, I rather expected that at that moment a special task force of the Japanese police would swing through our windows and pounce on us. It was a single noise of blaring warning sirens and a Japanese announcement that was completely incomprehensible to me.

After I shook the sleep away, I then saw the "Earthquake Warning" display on my lock screen and now at least knew what had happened. And I had learned that smartphones in Japan can do a bit more than elsewhere.

Over the next months and years, I heard the characteristic Japanese earthquake alarm over and over again, in the office, in restaurants, in bed. And to this day I'm conditioned to it - when I hear it in a movie, for example (I recommend the first episode of "Japan Sinks" on Netflix for this), I cringe and still instinctively look for the nearest table or shelter.

In Japan, an earthquake alarm is automatically issued when an earthquake exceeds an intensity of five on the Japanese seismic scale called “shindo” in an area that is likely to be affected by the quake. Shindo differs from the Richter scale used in the West. Shindo measures the intensity, or what people *feel* at a certain location, whereas the Richter scale measures the magnitude, or *energy* of the quake at a location. Since the radius of an earthquake cannot be predicted precisely in a few milliseconds, the area to be warned is chosen rather generously. Therefore, it is quite possible that all cell phones around you give an alarm and then nothing at all is felt.

Within Tokyo, we have also experienced several times that friends in different places of the city perceived a quake very differently. This depends on the exact position in relation to the epicenter of the quake, but also the nature of the ground in the area of the current stay, how high one is in a building height of stay as well as the type of building in which one is located.

During a very strong quake, the strongest in the ten years since the Fukushima disaster, the entire house creaked for a whole minute, the floors shook, the lamps swung up to the ceiling, and my wife sprinted to the children's room with the earthquake gear.

I myself was three miles down the road in a basement restaurant at this point and held on to the host's collection of grappa bottles without any major problems. Together, we were able to avoid any damage to the alcohol supply, and so I simply continued to eat afterwards and did not give any further thought to the supposedly small quake. It was not until an hour later, at the metro station, that I realized from the messages on all the monitors and the excited people around me how strong the tremors had been in most places.

How do you prepare for such an earthquake? There are many things you can do, but in the event of an earthquake, many things will probably turn out differently. Basically, Japan does a lot to prepare its citizens and all government institutions and bodies for earthquakes. Our children, for example, had earthquake training at daycare every eight weeks from the age of three. For this, each child had a kind of "pillow cap" that makes them look like a garden gnome. These caps are available in all classrooms. In the event of an earthquake, they are put over their heads, and with these protective caps they go under tables and benches for the duration of the quake. When the earthquake calms down, all the children go outside with their caps and gather in open areas.

In the event of very severe quakes, classes move on to the nearest earthquake shelter. These are usually secondary schools that are built to be earthquake-resistant and equipped with supplies for the population of the surrounding streets. There are also large additional shelters and emergency hospitals, for example in sports stadiums.

The shelter for our family and neighborhood would have been a school about five hundred yards away and the site of the 1964

Tokyo Olympic Games in Komazawa Park would have served as an emergency hospital for all adjacent neighborhoods, including helipads for the safe landing of rescue helicopters.

The Olympic site was about four miles away from us, but in front of our house and on every second or third street corner there were large rescue plans and signposts to the nearest shelters. Therefore, we knew exactly where to go in the event of a disaster and could also read the exact infrastructure of our shelter on the plans - for example, I learned about the helicopter landing pads I mentioned.

In addition to this emergency infrastructure, there is a great deal of information available and also training opportunities on how to properly prepare for earthquakes in your house or apartment. When we registered our residence, I was given a hundred and fifty page earthquake prevention manual by my municipality in perfect English - which is a real sensation, because detailed documents in perfect English on any subject are really very, very rare in Japan. After my shock at the first earthquake described above, I actually picked up this thick earthquake bible and read through it once from cover to cover with highlighter in hand. The result of my research was that I had to go shopping the next day.

Following the official advice, I bought enough bottled water for two weeks, a gas stove with enough gas cartridges, vacuum-packed ready-to-eat rice for two weeks (with a shelf life of five years), canned bread, canned cake with extra calories, dry sauces for the rice, an emergency toilet, a very sturdy crowbar, a spade, two fire extinguishers, lots of bandages, emergency medication, safety shoes for my wife and I, hard hats, helmet lamps, cut-resistant gloves, sturdy overalls and more.

All this, according to the manual, I should best store directly next to the bed or else directly at the exit of the house. Better to have one bag in each location so that it would always be available. Full of pride, I lugged home my disaster supplies, which cost around five hundred euros, and stowed them away in the closet and next to our beds in accordance with regulations. The next evening, over a beer and still proud of my emergency readiness, I told two Japanese friends about my perfect preparations. Both listened to me very quietly, then they snorted and said that I really was better prepared than any Japanese they knew in the greater Tokyo area. And maybe I should still join the volunteer fire department to learn more about active crisis prevention...

Fortunately, I never needed any of those things, and I still own thirty canned cakes in various flavors and an expiration date late in the 2030s. Who knows what it will be good for someday.

A rather unknown, but exciting and good possibility to get more intensively involved with earthquake preparation as a tourist are the earthquake training centers in Tokyo. There are such centers for all residents of the city, which you can easily visit even as a temporary visitor. One of them, located on the artificial island of Odaiba and quite easy to reach, simulates a severe earthquake with a staging like in Disneyworld. With "real" earthquake, falling walls, fire and darkness. After the quake, you have to "rescue" yourself through a course. This is definitely a very Japanese experience, it's free and a big hit with kids. At the same time, you learn a few important rules of conduct in case there really is a violent quake.

One last seismic anecdote: If you walk through Tokyo with your eyes open or take a cab or bus, you will see huge signs with a friendly grinning fish on them again and again above large multi-lane roads. This sign, which must be about one hundred square feet in size, indicates that you are on an emergency road. In the event of a severe earthquake, no cars are allowed to move here; the road is reserved for emergency vehicles. So far, so good. But what is the fish doing on the sign? This is because, according to legend, a giant catfish (Oonamazu) causes the earthquakes in Japan with movements of its body. Therefore, the catfish is a very obvious earthquake symbol for the Japanese - while we foreigners tend to think that the signs are advertisements for the next fish market.

The ongoing struggle of the Japanese with the weather

Nature is powerful in Japan. This is especially noticeable in the earthquakes just described. But also every other form of natural event always seemed to me a bit more intense, harder and more extreme in Japan than in Europe. When it rains, it pours. All day long. When the sun shines, it does so from a brilliant blue sky. And throughout the winter months in far warmer tones than on the kitschiest oil painting at the Italian restaurant around the corner. Wind usually only comes in the form of storms or typhoons. And snow falls in such huge quantities in some regions that hot spring water is simply continuously piped over the roads there so that they don't have to be constantly cleared.

And Japanese people love to deal with their weather. The weather report therefore takes up a considerable part of the news. Very friendly presenters stand in front of a map of Japan and explain the weather for the next few days with clouds, lightning, ice crystals and suns attached to wooden poles. These performances are very reminiscent of theater performances in elementary schools, but the weather forecast is usually very accurate. If rain is forecast for Tokyo at noon, then you can be sure that it will really get wet outside by half past twelve at the latest. And because it almost always pours, there are the same warnings every time: "The rain is dangerous. Large accumulations of water can form, in which cars sink. Landslides may occur. Please be very careful."

The same warning is given from spring to fall for every report of sun, slightly adapted: "The sun is dangerous. Anyone can get heat stroke at any time. Please be very careful. Stay indoors, stay in the shade, drink a lot of water." In fact, it is rare that the Japanese weather report is not garnished with eschatological warnings.

At the beginning of my time in Tokyo, I didn't realize how seriously the Japanese take the weather. But you learn quickly: a rain report means a wardrobe change before going to the office.

Put on boots, take an umbrella. And the whole city does the same. When rain is announced, rubber boots suddenly flash under the skirts of the ladies, transparent umbrellas hang on the arm of every (and I really mean EVERY) pedestrian from tall to short. When the first drop falls, millions of umbrellas pop up and cover streets with an almost closed blanket of plastic canopies. And the few unaware people without umbrellas, like me, can easily get one in any konbini for three hundred to five hundred yen.

However, the only idiot who had initially bought a white umbrella there instead of a transparent one was also me. While every Tokyoite with his transparent umbrella can see well where he is going and navigate halfway elegantly around the many other pedestrians around him, I was constantly ramming passers-by off the sidewalk or getting stuck on signs and corners. By the time I realized my mistake, I had made plenty of enemies. So I stumbled into the next konbini on my way, stuck my kamikaze umbrella in the umbrella stand at the entrance, and grabbed its transparent equivalent. Five hundred more yen, but definitely well invested.

By the way, people in Tokyo react to the sun in much the same way as they do to rain, only without rubber boots. As soon as the sun gets a little stronger, around March, many ladies wear a parasol. It looks like an umbrella, but for obvious reasons it is not transparent this time. Instead, it is covered with textile and its sides are often decorated with lace or little bobbles - which always gives parasols the charm of a British country party in the 19th century. Sporty ladies who are either walking or out with the dog like to wear gigantic parasols instead of the umbrella. These look like face shields worn a little too high against Corona, are darkly tinted and incredibly unattractive. But much loved.

I can explain that the sunshades make perfect sense with two examples. First, a tan in Japan is not a sign of good health, but an indication of barbaric lack of discipline in the face of the sun. The ideal of beauty in the country is quite clear - chalk white. And here, of course, the various mobile sunscreens are worth their weight in gold if you don't want to spend a fortune on all the whitening creams, masks and powders that beauty salons and drugstores offer.

On the other hand, the sun in Japan is really brutal and can massively affect you in the summer months. I have managed several times to get sunburned despite sunscreen with sun protection factor fifty. And items brought from Germany that are supposedly UV-resistant, such as a garden furniture cover, simply crumbled for us in Japan after the first summer.

Against the strong sun and very high heat in summer, there are other strongly widespread aids. While the ladies reach for the umbrella, almost all male Japanese I know help themselves with small cotton towels against the streams of sweat. The towels are available in every, you guessed it, konbini. Or alternatively, at sometimes horrendous prices, in various design boutiques. In addition to the wipes, there are small suction pads that you can stick under your arms. So that under no circumstances sweat is visible on the shirt. And for the really tough cases, there are cooling pads that you also stick under your armpits - although I imagine that to be more like torture.

Many craftsmen and gardeners walk around in the summer quite particularly protected in strikingly thick, long-sleeved jackets - at the sight of which one wonders at first whether this is supposed to represent perhaps a particularly perfidious kind of slow and agonizing suicide. At second glance, however, you realize that these are ventilated cooling vests. On the sides, two rapidly spinning fans constantly suck air into the inside of the jacket, which fills up like a cushion of air, which is why it looks so thick and cozy. In fact, the wearer is protected from the sun while being additionally and actively cooled by about ten degrees.

While these cooling vests are really worn exclusively by craftsmen, many other people hang electric fans around their necks to cool off in the summer. There are two main models. One is simply a handy little fan maybe fifteen centimeters in diameter that you wear around your neck with a cord. Above the battery, you can bend it smoothly. This allows the battery to rest on your chest, and the fan head can be tilted to blow gently or harshly into your face as needed.

More advanced are neck fans. They look like large DJ headphones that you rest on your shoulders and neck. Instead of the ear cups, there are two fans that blow air from the right and left around the head.

Travel and accommodation in Japan

How to find a good hotel in Japan and how not to

There are decent hotel chains all over Japan. One of them is known as "Dormy Inn". There, a night in a double room costs about $100, the hotels almost always have their own onsen and the standard is absolutely fine. But you can, and this is a uniquely Japanese phenomenon, walk right next door from your "Dormy Inn" into a hotel where time simply stood still sometime in the 80s. The place continues to run and is obviously booked. Yet everything there, from the rickety reception desk in dark brown walnut veneer to the clattering elevator to the completely yellowed and worn rooms, screams out loud: "Please: Tear me off!"

On a multi-day bike tour of Japan, we had booked all the hotels along our route in advance through the tour provider. The first night we slept in an old but beautiful ryokan. The second night we wanted to spend at a big volcanic lake. Every evening there was a big fireworks display on the lake, accordingly there were numerous hotels on the shore. It was a well-known excursion place with thousands of guests who wanted to take a romantic trip here. The large number of guests probably meant that there was little pressure to renovate the place. No one there spoke English, and we didn't speak Japanese at the time, so our extremely friendly receptionist led us to the room on the tenth or fifteenth floor, way up in the hotel anyway. Behind the door opened a yellow cave, a room nicotine-colored from the flooring all the way up to the ceiling paneling. The ravages of time had managed to make the carpet, curtains, walls and the fixed formica nightstand shimmer in the exact same hue. This symphony in yellow was broken only by the built-in radio alarm clock with an analog folding display (does anyone remember these from their childhood?), which was set into the headboard of the bed in rich brown and showed the time there presumably from 1965 until about 1985. Then it stopped, but had not been replaced in the last thirty years. In the middle of this room stood our bed, supplemented by two bedside lamps firmly screwed to the side panels. There was a palm-sized hole in the lampshade of one of the lamps. A fat cockroach was sitting on the right sheet.

The cockroach was immediately discovered by our nice receptionist and disposed of by hand, bowing deeply. A miracle, because normally these cute little animals dart in no time to the next dark corner - my theory is that this specimen had already decided to die in the middle of our bed in view of the dreariness of the room.

We were so overwhelmed by all the impressions in the first thirty seconds (ancient room, broken lamp, cockroach, etc.), that we said nothing at first. After we came back to ourselves, we called the organizer of our bike tour and lamented our woes: room not renovated for fifty years, cockroach on the bed and it stinks like an ashtray. He consulted with the reception and called us back: the hotel was fully booked, the room was up to hotel standard, and the smell would be taken care of right away.

A few minutes later, there was a knock at the door. Our friendly receptionist and cockroach disposer was there again. Bowing deeply, he walked into the room, took several clearly audible breaths, and seemed to understand that it didn't exactly smell like white orchid. He then whipped out a spray bottle and began spraying every corner of our room. With some sort of scent killer room scent. Every ten sprays he would straighten up, audibly suck in the air again and spray the next corner. It was an incredible show. The man was so sincerely trying to help us that it was touching. At the same time, he didn't change anything at all about the root of the problem, but just tinkered with the symptoms with a lot of huffing and puffing. But he demonstrated impressively, and certainly very face-savingly, that he cared about the welfare of his guests. Even if he or his management had put them up in an absolute dump.

After ten minutes, our room smelled like a drugstore. Our receptionist took in a few more breaths of air, looked at us questioningly, and pointed his thumb upward. "Okay?" What should we do. We said "Okay," thanked him for the dedicated spraying of what must have been a quart of unknown chemicals in our bedroom, and then went to get drunk.

Many travelers to Japan can tell similar stories. But it does not have to be like our bike tour. You can rent a double room in large cities for fifty to sixty dollars a night and get a clean and neat home with bathroom and air conditioning. The usual booking platforms will point you in the right direction. In addition to Western sites like booking.com, the national "Rakuten Travel" platform, which is available in serviceable English, is also a good option in Japan.

However, such a room, including the bathroom, will only be a good ten square meters in size and, unfortunately, will not look like you imagined a Japanese room to look like. This means that anyone who dreamed of calligraphed pictures, Zen elements, tatami mats and lots of bamboo in the small front garden by the entrance will be disappointed here. But if you want to be on the road all day, especially in Tokyo, and just need a cozy bed, these cheap business hotels are great to use.

It is more difficult outside the capital. Here, of course, there are business hotels everywhere, but the condition of many of these hostels decreases the farther away from Tokyo you are, in my experience.

You wouldn't expect to find a large number of completely worn-out hotels in Japan, and many travelers end up staying in such places, at least on their first trip to the country. And this in turn gives rise to the often-heard and widespread opinion on the Internet that hotels in Japan are terribly old and completely overpriced. To avoid such experiences, it only helps to look at current photos of real visitors and to read current, English-language reviews of Western visitors on the booking platforms in detail. If you spend some time on this, you should be able to avoid most junk hotels. It is also recommended to pay attention to whether the comments mention that only certain rooms or room categories are renovated. It happens quite often that every year only a few rooms are renewed and a hotel thus offers very different experiences...

If you want something prettier than just staying in a business hotel, the game actually gets more complicated. The traditional ryokan hotels offer the most intensely Japanese experience, and I'll go into detail on that in the next chapter. However, the transition between regular hotels and ryokans is blurred in reality. For example, there are very many hotels with on-site onsen, which immediately adds flair to the stay and was always indispensable for me. No onsen, no overnight stay. Especially since you can wash there in peace, whereas the bathroom in your own room is usually so small that your butt is practically in the sink while showering.

Beyond the onsen, many hotels have "Western-style rooms" with carpet and beds, and alternatively "Japanese-style rooms" with tatami floors and futons or at least very low mattresses. Booking the Japanese rooms here makes the whole overnight stay feel a little more exotic and special.

Hotels renovated in recent years often offer rooms with their own small onsen bath, preferably on the terrace or balcony. Now those rooms are an absolute hit, especially with children. After all, the real onsen is, as those more attentive readers recall, a purification spa, not a playground for children. Accordingly, you can scrub and soak there with your offspring, but splashing and noises are absolute no-nos. On our own terrace, things look quite different. Our children have spent many fun-filled hours in the onsen, sinking Playmobil pirate ships and enthusiastically trying again and again to somehow drain the entire tub.

But even without children I recommend shelling out for an in-room onsen bath at least once. The additional price for these rooms is somewhere between fifty and one hundred and fifty dollars. These rooms are more often than not renovated more recently and somewhat larger than standard rooms. In return, you can look at the Japanese starry sky outside at night in the warm water, look at the sea or listen to the sounds of the forest, depending on the location of the hotel. That experience by itself is certainly worth something!

Often there is also a "Private Onsen" not attached to a single room, but available for everybody. This means that in addition to the large onsen for all guests, you can privately rent a particularly pretty onsen for half an hour or a whole hour. This is done by many Japanese families, for the reasons described above - with children it is much more relaxed to bathe together as a family. And here you can also bathe together as a couple, while the public onsen is separated by gender and thus anything but communicative.

If you want to reserve such a private onsen, you should already make that clear at check-in. Usually the rush is great, and as so often in life the same rule applies: first come, first bathe.

And what if, despite the best preparation, you end up in a run-down hotel? At least there is the consolation that this night will probably be the one you will still tell your friends and acquaintances about for many years to come ...

The unique Japan experience: staying overnight in a ryokan

Ryokan translates roughly as "traveler's inn," and that's exactly what it is: a traditional form of Japanese inn established for many centuries. The oldest existing ryokan stands in Yamanashi Prefecture, northwest of Fuji-san, and has been in continuous operation there since the year 705 CE. With over 1,300 years of operation, it is considered the oldest hotel in the world still in existence, and the second oldest incorporated business in the world.

Regardless of whether it's a modern new building or a traditional wooden house, ryokans are always more traditional and often a bit more hospitable than ordinary hotels. The traveler comes here not only to spend the night, but also to clean, relax and eat. And especially in smaller ryokans, the traveler is often treated like a friend of the family, not like a paying customer passing through. Basically, you can think of ryokans as a form of wellness hotel that has existed since the early Middle Ages, coupled with a great deal of Japanese hospitality and cultural care.

One of the most beautiful ryokan experiences we had was during a hike on the Nakasendo. This is the old, very remote and over long stretches wildly romantic riding and hiking route between Tokyo and Kyoto. We had been walking there all day through pelting rain. It was chilly, maybe 50 degrees Fahrenheit, and on a foggy November day we arrived at nightfall in Otsumago - an ancient hamlet in the Japanese Alps made up almost entirely of historic wooden houses. A large paper lantern stood in front of one of the many buildings made of jet-black wood, directing us to the entrance of our lodging for the night. A four hundred year old ryokan.

To enter from the street through the old and low sliding door, we had to stoop low. Behind it was a small hallway of tamped earth, where we took off our dripping jackets and backpacks. And of course our soaked shoes.

Rarely was it so much fun to slip into provided slippers. They were the same as almost everywhere in Japan, simple plastic slippers. But they felt like warmth and security after the day in disastrous weather. Even more, however, was the wood fire that provided homey warmth a few feet away from us. Just two wooden steps built on the clay ground separated us from the irori, a fireplace sunk into the ground on our right hand side. There we first sat down on the surrounding tatami mats, got a hot tea from our hosts and slowly warmed up again.

A little later we moved into our rooms on the upper floor. According to our landlords, they had not been changed in over two hundred years, except for the addition of power strips in the walls. The rooms were along a narrow hallway. On both sides bordered by beautifully painted paper walls, so-called Fusuma.

Traditionally, Japanese interiors are bordered by two different types of paper walls. Shoji walls consist of a visible wooden frame and are covered with white paper. They are translucent and separate the interior of the house from the outside world, similar to frosted glass panels. Fusuma are thicker, opaque, often wallpapered or painted, and separate bedrooms, for example.

At the end of the corridor, our host pushed apart two fusuma to the right, and we could enter our rooms. They were compact with a size of six tatami, that is, each laid out with six tatami mats. Unfortunately, I cannot say exactly how big they were. Because, unfortunately, we were hiking in the vicinity of the "tatami border." In the Tokyo area and further east, the traditional tatami measurement is 35 by 69 inches. In Kyoto and the west, however, it is 38 by 75 inches. And since I didn't have a folding rule with me, it unfortunately remained unclear on which half of the tatami equator we were at that moment ...

In our rooms the futons were already rolled out, very cozy mattresses with thick down comforters on them. The latter were also necessary, because later in the evening frost was reported. And between us and the freezing night was only a millimeter-thin layer of paper.

Later, however, there was a little more protection from the weather. In the evening, heavy wooden sliding doors were closed on the outside facade, so that there was another layer of separation between us and the outside. In addition, we were given a kerosene burner with an electric fan, as I described in the chapter on Japanese houses. However, these devices turn off after two to three hours for safety reasons, so they really only provide additional coziness when you fall asleep and then in the morning when you turn them on again.

After we had undressed in our room and put on the prepared yukatas, a sort of traditional Japanese equivalent to a tracksuit, we made our way to the onsen, which was located behind a small garden. We changed from our house slippers to garden slippers, walked a few meters through a romantic moss garden, and entered the onsen, my wife on the left with one child, I on the right with the other. We were alone, and so we washed and scrubbed ourselves till we were very relaxed and then cooked ourselves in the small but fine mineral water pool.

Cleaned from top to bottom and, most importantly, wonderfully warmed up, we went straight from here to dinner, which was served in a small dining room for all fifteen or so guests at the same time – 7:00pm on the dot. There was a classic kaiseki menu. I describe kaiseki in detail in the food chapter. In our case, it was a very tasty succession of lots of autumn vegetables from the surrounding mountains, various kinds of game, and a little river fish. In addition, I enjoyed a few bottles of beer, as did all of the other guests seated nearby. Somehow no one drank sake here, and my ice-cold Asahi went very well with the food.

At half past eight, the last course was served, in the form of large portions of rice to guarantee that the guests would get their fill. And at just before 9:00pm, all the visitors got up and went to their rooms so that the host family could tidy up in peace.

So we too climbed up to our floor, crept past the other rooms, from which not a single word could be heard despite the thin walls, and lay down as quietly as possible in our cozy beds. A perfect ryokan evening came to an end, and tomorrow, after an extensive morning dip in the beautiful garden onsen, we would quickly have our small Japanese breakfast of fish and rice before hitting the slopes again.

Of course, not every ryokan in Japan was or is quite as historic, romantic and beautiful as the stay described here. In fact, there is a very wide variety of ryokans, from very old and traditional houses to large and almost anonymous ryokan hotels that accommodate hundreds of guests at a time. The equipment and service of both old and new ryokans can be very modern and downright luxurious, but also very simple. Therefore, it is always worthwhile to read reviews carefully before booking. What all ryokans have in common, however, are the following things:

There will always be an onsen. Mostly with real mineral water, sometimes with heated city water. However, this is - strictly regulated by law – detailed at the time of booking, just as the number, type and temperature of the available baths.

In addition, a lavish dinner will always be included in the rather high booking price. Often this is a very nice kaiseki menu, which is served to the guests in the best case in their own room. First you wash yourself properly in the onsen, then you dress in the prepared yukata, and afterwards a multi-course Japanese feast is served directly in your own room or in a communal dining room, as I will describe in a moment. During this room service process, by the way, the waiters, regardless of age, consistently slide on their knees across the tatami mats from the entrance of the room to the dining table. This is somewhat irritating and was honestly uncomfortable for me. But well, that's the way tradition wants it. And my dear readers have probably already noticed that tradition is extremely important in Japan.

If there is no room service or it is already fully booked, food is served in a dining room. Sometimes in individual alcoves, sometimes with other guests within sight and hearing. It also happens that the food is offered as a buffet. However, this is then quite far from the actual idea of a ryokan, and I would try to avoid such hotels. Buffet food can also be very good, but it is not the experience for which one books a ryokan for a lot of money.

Besides onsen and kaiseki dinners, you will almost always stay in a classic Japanese living room and bedroom. The floor is covered with tatami mats, futons for sleeping, a wall niche ("*tokonoma*") with a piece of art for viewing in it, a small table with seat cushions, a kettle and some tea. Very rarely, there are also "Western-style rooms" in a ryokan, but I would really only book those if I needed a high bed because of health problems.

Many Japanese acquaintances of ours rarely went to a ryokan, perhaps once a year for one or two nights, as a couple or family event. That's what most guests do, and that's what many ryokans are geared toward. Less a hostel for wet hikers than a feel-good temple of Japanese hospitality and culture in which one can enjoy oneself very well, with extensive onsen visits and subsequent feasts with lots of delicious alcohol.

Since food is so important, booking the right menu is often more time-consuming than choosing the nicest room. On many websites of ryokans you have to fight your way, unfortunately often only in Japanese, through endless descriptions of the evening's menu. And often only after very intensive study of the texts do you understand why one accommodation option should be five thousand yen more expensive than the other. Aha, instead of a lobster sashimi for the starter there is an Ise lobster sashimi! That is, with lobster caught off the Ise Peninsula. Which, you can guess, in a certain month is considered the best lobster in Japan and thus in the world at this time by all connoisseurs of Japan (meaning virtually every inhabitant of the country ...).

Generally speaking, ryokans are very expensive. To a certain extent, this can be explained by the two full meals per night stay, including the luxurious kaiseki menu. But even if you include this at Tokyo restaurant prices, ryokans are still no bargain. My theory is that the typical short booking of only one or two nights a year is the deciding factor here. As a result, customers simply don't care about the price to some extent. If the local population only treats itself to a day or a weekend at the ryokan once a year, then it no longer makes a decisive difference whether this excursion costs thirty thousand or thirty-five thousand yen per person. It's probably the same as a trip to an amusement park: If we do something like Disneyland once in a while, then we really treat ourselves to it instead of watching every yen.

Very nice impressions of various exclusive ryokans, most of them really expensive and much more an inspiration than a recommendation for booking, can be found at ryokancollection.com.

Camping in Japan - advanced tent adventures

Is there anything more beautiful than sitting with your children in front of your own tent in the evening, eating rice freshly cooked over the fire and listening to the chirping of the cicadas? Yes. When it's over 100 degrees Fahrenheit in the evening, the tent feels like it's ten degrees higher, there's rice for the fourth day in a row, and the cicadas are so loud that it's almost impossible to have a normal conversation.

Camping in Japan was not nice in all respects. We had fled Tokyo for Hokkaido in August, where it was supposed to be fifteen degrees colder and much less humid than in the capital. But we were probably unlucky, took the weather from our home with the ferry - and brought the blistering hot and humid midsummer with us to the north of Japan.

But even though our tent adventure started way too hot and finally ended, I'll just touch on it, with a three-day typhoon and our escape to a hotel, the days at a Japanese campsite were again a special experience worth telling.

Beforehand: We had pitched our tent on a fairly new, very well-kept and modern site at a reservoir in Hokkaido. Close to the area around Furano, where many tourists visit on a Hokkaido trip to see the large fruit and lavender farms here - because there is not too much to see in Hokkaido.

On this northernmost large island of Japan apparently no one spoke English, or at least no one wanted to admit it. But thanks to my wife's now advanced knowledge of Japanese, we had reserved a nice campsite right on the water and were very kindly welcomed there on a Wednesday evening.

That first evening, 48 of the 50 or so tent sites were vacant. A lone tent stood in one corner of the site and ours in the other. So we relaxed and set up our temporary abode, a family tent purchased online from the discount sports store. In addition, we had our much-used beach pavilion as a shade for eating with us, as well as all the little accessories that make camping pleasant: Folding chairs, a folding table and so on.

The next day the other tent left in the morning. We were all alone in the late morning and drove our car to look at a lavender farm in the area.

When we returned in the afternoon, there were a good twenty tents on the site, and tents without exception - camping trailers or even motor homes seem to be almost non-existent in Japan. Whether this is due to the problematic parking situation or simply to the somewhat limited radius of operation when the home country is completely surrounded by the Pacific Ocean, I have not been able to find out.

The tents around us shared two characteristics for the most part: they were very large compared to ours. And they were almost without exception from the same company, "Snow Peak".

Snow Peak is a Japanese phenomenon that has only reached Europe to a small extent. The company was founded in 1958 in Japan and is not only the Mercedes among the tents, but a very high-quality, very expensive supplier of pretty much everything you need for camping and storage. In recent years, the company has expanded very successfully into the U.S., which is why I assume that sooner or later it will also become more present in Europe.

The living spaces of our neighbors were fundamentally different from our model. As I said, they were larger. They also had no folds. They simply stood there like monoliths. Tautly stretched, robust, shiny - beautiful. My gaze wandered from our somewhat wrinkled plastic cave with its beach pavilion in front to the camping temples of all our neighbors, which were completed in strict, dignified harmony, and I wondered what they might think about our accommodation.

The next morning, around eleven o'clock, we were again completely alone on the campsite. All the other tents had been taken down and their owners had already left.

We also left again, this time to look at a mystically discolored blue lake nearby. Which, while very photogenic, is actually man-made, surprisingly small, and saturated with aluminum hydroxide due to a freak of nature. But that's another story.

In the evening we returned to our campsite and once again it was full to capacity. Friday night is camping night, and Saturday, of course, too.

Camping might not be the most popular sport in Japan, but it is a well-liked little escape from everyday life. This escape is made by all those who have to work on the weekend during the week on the eve of the day off. And everyone else does it, as expected, on the weekend. But rather briefly, aiming at making the most of the one or two days off, not for a vacation lasting several days.

Young couples especially like to go camping for obvious reasons. Unlike at a love hotel (more on that in the next chapter), you can use the tent for twenty-four hours at no extra charge. Accordingly, we usually saw our younger neighbors only at an early dinner, and then they preferred to spend the rest of the camping adventure in their tents rather than outside around the campfire.

The other obvious user group of the campground was young families with several children. In very many hotels and all ryokans I know of, children are included at high rates in Japan. Therefore, a short vacation with the family is a really expensive undertaking. Where the offspring, despite the high price, must be quiet and considerate most of the time, instead of being able to let off steam. Here, of course, camping offers much more possibilities, and so chummy families often book the log cabins available at many campsites and organize quite wild children's playtimes there with lots of games, inflatable pools and nightly fireworks.

The third group of Japanese campsite users was a bit more surprising for us: pet owners. Various campsites around us turned into small pet farms by means of foldable fences and separate dog tents. Happy couples lived there, happily playing with their four-legged friends. So that the dogs did not have to suffer with the mad temperatures, large fans and high quantity water bowls were in use. In addition, there were baskets for each little creature to cuddle and sleep, and in at least one case in our neighborhood even freshly cooked dinner for each little fellow.

What was particularly impressive about camping in Japan: of course, the consideration. Apart from a few children playing quietly, it was peaceful mealtime from eight o'clock in the evening. All guests gathered around their foldable Snow Peak stainless steel fireplaces, where almost without exception the female fellow travelers had been busy chopping and roasting for the last two hours. From nine o'clock then everywhere people were drinking, and certainly not in small quantities, but in complete silence. And around ten o'clock all guests disappeared whispering in their tents. Throughout the evenings, even on Friday and Saturday with the campsite fully booked, the only loud perceptible sound on the site was the noise of the cicadas.

Would we go camping in Japan again? Most certainly. But no more in hot August. And probably not in Hokkaido in general. In recent years, the brown bear population there has grown massively, and at many campsites, including ours, signs warn at every turn against visits from some big furry friends.

But at a nice lake in the Japanese Alps, with a view of a volcano and a natural onsen right next to the campsite, I would pitch my tent again at any time for a weekend. This time, however, not the plastic bag from the discount store, but a stately Japanese tent palace. Only a week after our vacation, I was already in the Snow Peak store in Tokyo to upgrade accordingly.

How and why to book a Love Hotel

Love hotels are a Japanese institution that are hard to miss. At highway interchanges, there are often adventurous buildings in wild shapes that remotely resemble ocean liners, a Roman amphitheater or a medieval castle. But not perfectly imitated as in a theme park, they are usually somewhat crudely and awkwardly planted in the landscape - people take photos here more out of wonder than admiration.

In the cities, love hotels don't necessarily look as imaginative as they do along the highway, but they do like to have a few pseudo-Roman columns at the entrance or a small fountain made of cast stone next to the facade. Again, beautiful is different..

So what is the benefit of these hotels? As the name suggests, they are primarily for intimate encounters. However, and this may come as a surprise, not primarily for paid love. The main user group of love hotels in Japan are married couples.

Now the interested reader may ask: Yes, don't they have a home? Yes, of course they do. But it's usually cramped and often the children sleep in the parents' bedroom. The husband's mother may also live in the household. And in addition to the apartments being cramped, the walls are also thin. That's why it's better to retreat for a few hours, and the perfect place for that is the convenient love hotel.

In addition to married couples, of course, here you can find a lot of expectant couples or simply couples who very often live with their parents until their own wedding and also have no peace there.

In addition, the love hotels serve as workplaces for employees from the aforementioned "delivery health" studios, who provide the equivalent to room service here on an hourly basis.

Are these hotels reserved only for lovers? Not at all! As a rule, anyone can rent a room here, importantly, both for a few hours or for a whole night. Often, the night tariff is not that expensive, and thus the last important group of customers is addressed: Partygoers who have missed the train late at night.

In Tokyo, for example, the last trains leave around 12:30am. After that, there are no trains till around 4:00am. Those who go out in the evening usually start so early that he or she can comfortably get home on one of the last trains. However, if you really want to party and dance in a big club, you will take the last trains into town and then party for at least three hours until the trains start running again. By the way, this is also the reason why Japanese clubs don't get emptier between midnight and four o'clock. You can hardly get away anyway, so you step on the gas and party on.

But if you still want to go to bed, you have two options: take a sinfully expensive cab back to the suburbs or rent a room at a love hotel. After midnight, the latter are often even cheaper, you can get a fairly large and very clean room from 50 dollars, and fill it up with two to four friends, all fully dressed, laying out in the huge bed and to sleep off the long night. The next morning, the train goes home early, clothes are changed, and off everyone goes to the university or to work.

Since the big topic of love is seen as a private matter in Japan and is also somewhat shameful to speak about in general, love hotels are bastions of privacy. If there are parking spaces, they are fenced off. According to reports, in the better establishments a parking attendant even hangs cloths over the license plates of each freshly parked car so that absolute anonymity is maintained in the parking lot as well.

At the reception, you can either check in directly via a booking computer or do so at a counter with a privacy screen. You can only see the receptionist's hands while you discreetly slide your money or credit card through a slot.

The rooms themselves make a short visit to love hotel quite an opportunity to collect funny photos for Instagram. A huge TV with a large order menu usually awaits you here. You can order everything you could need in such a hotel via this screen. In addition to starting a wide variety of streaming videos, you can order various drinks, which are then placed in front of the door a few minutes later. But toy boxes are also available, which can be used to make the time for two a bit more imaginative. And, a highlight in the land of manga: very often there is also a large selection of costumes. Nurse costumes, nun costumes, various manga hero costumes or simply cat costumes – everything is online and just a click away from your room door.

Here, as a visitor, you can now really dig deep into Japanese subcultures and finally try how you look like dressed up as Sailor Moon, for example.

Do you have to have stayed at a Love Hotel? No, definitely not. But is it worth a short visit? I would say yes, to add a very special Japanese institution to one's travelogues. And if you dare to wear the costumes, you'll have some truly unique photos up your sleeve. Whether you upload them to social media or keep them for yourself is up to you.

The food in Japan

What you need to know about the best cuisine in the world

Anthony Bourdain, the late chef and journalist whom I adore, once said about food in Tokyo: "I love Tokyo. If I had to eat only in one city for the rest of my life, Tokyo would be it. Most chefs I know would agree with me." (Anthony Bourdain, "Parts Unknown" S2E8, 2013)

Nowhere in the world can you eat better, more varied and more accomplished food than in Japan. Japanese cuisine all by itself justifies a flight halfway around the world. My idea of a perfect short vacation is to simply fly to Tokyo and eat two to three meals every day in restaurants of my choice. I don't need any museums, temples or sightseeing there. Just maybe a treadmill and a personal trainer to keep me from turning into a sumo wrestler during my week-long binge.

What makes the food in Japan so uniquely good? That is a complex question to which there is no single answer. On the one hand, there is the variety of typical Japanese food. Everyone knows sushi. Sashimi, too. Then we have ramen, tempura, udon and soba as still familiar but somewhat more advanced dishes. Followed by okonomiyaki, onigiri, mochi, yakitori and kaiseki for Japan connoisseurs. And then come katsudon, curry, takoyaki, tonkatsu, tofu dishes of all stripes, and many, many more not necessarily known outside Japan, but which are the backbone of home cooking, cafeteria food, and many simple restaurants and izakayas.

Each of these meals is simply delicious. I can't say it any other way: Food in Japan simply tastes good. And what should you absolutely try as a traveler to Japan? Of course, everything!

I am not a specialized journalist for upscale gastronomy, and in the German equivalent of Food and Wine magazine I honestly only ever looked at the pictures. But I will do my best to make my esteemed readers more familiar with the basic pillars of Japanese cuisine.

Of course, you know what **sushi** is. In Japan, sushi ranges from very cheap to very expensive. Qualitatively, however, even cheap restaurants are often much better than the majority of sushi in the rest of the world. There tends to be much more nigiri sushi in Japan, where there is a larger piece of fish on a small bed of rice so that the customer can experience the freshness and quality of the fish very clearly. There aren't so many sushi rolls (maki) where less or even lower quality fish can be used, and rolls in Japan are much less complicated than what many Western easters may be familiar with. Further, foreign rolls often use so much sauce and mayonnaise that it drowns out the entire interior. The heavily seasoned "Crispy Hot Philadelphia Avocado Tuna Roll" variations that are so familiar are all American creations, where a distinct sushi culture emerged in the 1980s.

Unlike "western sushi", salmon and tuna are far from dominant in Japanese sushi making. If you are in the island kingdom, then you should therefore enjoy the variety of fish and seafood that you can suddenly eat here as sushi. Some visitors avoid ebi (raw shrimp) as it is thought to be slimey. Also, ika (squid), which has a very firm texture and is quite tough to chew if not really prepared perfectly tends to be overlooked as well. Both are delicious when prepared in Japan, so please try them!

Uni (sea urchin) is also not preferred by tourists, but I highly recommend trying this delicacy in high class restaurants. In cheap sushi, uni is also still okay, but it then tastes very strongly of fish, which is not for everyone's tastes. And finally, there is shirako. This tastes great as long as you don't know what it is. At my first shirako nigiri, all of my Japanese friends looked deeply into their sake cups in embarrassment while I chewed blithely. Only to ask me immediately after swallowing if I had enjoyed it and if everything was okay. Shirako are the sperm of cod. For simplicity, you eat them with the whole sperm sac of the fish, and it looks a bit like a creamy rice pudding or a pale, gelatinous sausage. Or a white brain? In any case, it tastes mild, a bit like pudding. But again, the better the restaurant, the finer the taste. And the cheaper the restaurant... well, you get the picture. But remember: Even cheap sushi in Japan is never bad.

Ramen is actually a Chinese dish, but like many other fantastic dishes in Japan, it was first imported, then tweaked, and then perfected over many years. How do you perfect a bowl of noodle soup? There are a surprising number of ways to tinker with and adjust this seemingly simple dish, and every single one of them is tweaked in Japan's ubiquitous ramen shops. Day after day, always a little more perfect. For those who want to delve deeply into the subject, I strongly recommend the nearly two-hour independent film "Tampopo" about desire, pleasure and the perfect bowl of ramen.

If you don't want to put yourself through that, just imagine the components of one of those steaming bowls. First, there are noodles. But what kind of noodles, how thick are the noodles, what is the dough made of and what is the maximum age of the dough when the noodle is cooked? What consistency should the noodle have? All of these are deliberate decisions by a ramen chef that make up the individual style of his small restaurant and are evaluated down to the smallest detail in Japanese ramen guides and ramen apps by the discerning clientele. Unfortunately, these are only ever available in Japanese.

Because the consistency of ingredients is valued very, very highly in Japan and is an important part of the characteristics of every meal, you can often order soup and noodles separately in good ramen restaurants. After all, the noodles continue to cook in the boiling hot broth even in the customer's bowl. So the first bites of noodles will have a different consistency than the last, and to prevent this extremely unfortunate process, there is the separate serving method for consistency purists.

Back to our bowl of ramen. Along with the perfect noodles, there is the perfect broth. My favorite was the broth from a seven-seat ramen shack near Ookayama Station. This place served tonkotsu ramen, which is a broth based on pork, in particular pork bones, that simmers for anywhere from 12-24 hours and produces a fabulously creamy, intense broth. Additionally, and a bit more unusually, several fish heads and bones were simmering along in my ramen master's huge pot. This produced such an intense, delicious combination of flavors that I would have immediately marketed the broth alone as a sauce by itself given the chance.

Ramen broths range from light and rather watery (for example, like salt-based shio ramen) to heavy and creamy (common with tonkotsu ramen), and the flavor explosion of the creamy soup at this little store was phenomenal. The noodles were rather thin, had a lot of bite, the broth was as described, plus a soft boiled egg (this is a classic ingredient, but again, the absolutely perfect consistency of the creamy sweet egg yolk makes all the difference), a crispy sheet of nori made from green seaweed (pay attention to how different crispy nori can be from one type to the next), some delicious slices of roast pork (again, absolutely typical of tonkotsu ramen, but of course the taste varies with the quality) and a pinch of scallions.

Of course, there are also huge ramen chains, and they are not bad at all for getting to know the different varieties. Very well-known and only medium-sized is "Ichiran", where you can get to know very good ramen.

But for me, nothing beats the small restaurants. They often look kind of dingy and creepy, and maybe all five to ten seats are taken when you arrive. Then you just have to wait a little. Meanwhile, you should already buy the ticket for the desired dish at the payment machine near the entrance with the help of Google Translate (and almost always pay cash, so make sure you bring1,000 yen bills). Once you've bought your ticket, you can immediately occupy the next free seat.

As soon as you're seated, the host/chef will hand you a glass or carafe of water. You then simply hand him your ticket and watch as your bowl of ramen takes shape in a matter of minutes from fresh noodles, steaming yokes and lots and lots of running water.

Tempura is at first glance vegetables and fish deep-fried in beer batter. At second glance, the batter is paper-thin, coating the ingredients only very delicately. And at third glance, good tempura elevates the art of deep-frying to absolute star cuisine level.

Tempura is often offered in soba noodle restaurants, where the buckwheat noodles are accompanied by vegetables prepared as tempura. Or the crispy tempura ingredients lie on a bowl of rice, can be crunched away and complement the soft consistency of the rice with crunchy accents - as I said, the feeling in one's mouth as they eat is very important in Japanese cuisine.

It's easy to tell whether a restaurant specializing purely in tempura is any good as soon as you walk in. There is simply no smell of deep-frying fat. Never. Perfect oil, perfect temperature and constant cleaning of the fat from all crumbs and dough residues lead to completely scent-free frying - before we lived in Japan, I didn't even know that such a thing was possible.

I had my best tempura ever one evening in April with my friend Peter at a small eight-seat restaurant called Tempura Miyashiro in Nakameguro. What was celebrated here before our eyes for over two and a half hours was simply the highest culinary art.

A cube of beef tenderloin, so pink it literally melted in your mouth, wrapped in a shiso leaf, prepared with a paper-thin tempura crust. A monkfish nigiri covered with fresh uni/sea urchin, but served not on rice, but on a nori sheet deep-fried for just a few seconds. Sardines, which watched us curiously from a large fishbowl for the first half of the meal, were crisp-fried within twenty seconds and served alongside some radish on our plates. The hard shell at the end of a huge shrimp, discarded hundreds of times in my life so far, was here lightly glazed with tempura batter and deep-fried to the point of being so crispy that you wouldn't have wanted to eat anything else all evening. And to top it all off: a spear of asparagus.

This may sound very strange now, but the most impressive dish was really this one spear of green asparagus. Deep-fried and coated in tempura batter, it lay before us - and our chef told us to enjoy it in three sections, starting at the tip. He had the last four inches still raw in front of him and said he would prepare these in parallel and a little longer. Each of the three bites into this asparagus spear was a revelation. It was the essence of asparagus, more so than any cooked pound of asparagus will ever be for me. And to top it off, there was the extra-long deep-fried end piece, which if you had prepared it in your own kitchen, you might have tossed into the compost pile for being too woody. Here it was the crowning glory of the asparagus festival, hot and crispy and soft and tender and just bursting with flavors and aroma. It was fantastic! I'll spare a description of the other ten courses here, and also the accompanying sake we enjoyed. All I could say following that meal was Amen. There were now two distinct world's of fried for me: one from before and one from after this meal. This new world is so light, flavorful, and artful that I really don't want to go back to the old one.

Soba and udon are typical Japanese noodles that you encounter again and again. Soba probably more often, because there are many soba-ya, or soba restaurants, but some of them, confusingly, also serve udon dishes. – So what is it about these two types of noodles?

Soba are thin, brown noodles, similar to a whole grain spaghetti. However, they are always made from buckwheat, which is not a true grain and therefore gluten-free - but can cause other allergic reactions in some people.

Soba can be served cold or hot, with the cold version being a particularly excellent option in the hot Japanese summer months. The soba noodles are served on a wooden tray and accompanied by a bowl of soba tsuyu, a mixture of soy sauce, a sweet rice wine sauce called mirin and dashi. Dashi is the all-purpose weapon of Japanese cuisine, a clear broth made from seaweed and fish, which one encounters in many recipes and in every Japanese supermarket in a variety of forms.

The cold soba are dipped into the sauce one mouthful at a time with chopsticks and slurped up with relish. This is often accompanied by tempura and some seasoning ingredients such as spring onions.

After the meal, in many restaurants, another kettle of very hot water is brought to the table - this is the water in which the soba were cooked. It is poured on with the rest of the soba tsuyu so that you can drink it as a hot soup. I didn't know this on my first visit to a soba restaurant and held out my teacup to the waitress with a friendly smile - which visibly embarrassed the old lady.

Udon is much thicker than soba, being made of wheat flour, and has a glossy white sheen. Udon is often eaten like a stew, with various ingredients together with the noodles in a bowl. Udon could definitely be used to cook any stew that incorporates noodles, like chicken noodle soup. In simple terms, the formula is often: udon plus vegetables plus broth plus an extra like meat or crispy tempura cracklings.

Okonomiyaki are described as "Japanese pancakes" in all the guidebooks I know, but that's pretty much nonsense. Okonomiyaki is not made in a pan, does not consist mainly of batter and is not sweet (or a breakfast food). Rather, okonomiyaki is a pile of white cabbage with some batter and quite random ingredients from the categories of fish, meat, shellfish and vegetables. And there's always a very heavy drizzle of okonomiyaki sauce and mayonnaise on top.

The okonomiyaki, by the way, is also the ultimate proof that Japanese cuisine is neither light nor low-fat nor calorie-conscious. On the contrary, despite the high vegetable content, one portion of okonomiyaki is a really powerful and high-calorie meal. In contrast, a hot dog with fries seems much lighter. But this Japanese cabbage fritter really is delicious. And in many restaurants, it's an especially fun meal because you can fry it yourself. You either sit at the counter in front of a huge skillet, called a teppan, or there is a teppan built into the dining table itself.

The procedure can vary a little depending on the order, but basically the preparation always follows the same pattern. After choosing your favorite option from the menu, you get one or two bowls with the nicely arranged ingredients. This is also the right moment to look at your waiter or waitress with sad, desperate eyes – and then they will prepare the food in front of your eyes so you don't have to do anything yourself.

Or you simply go courageously to work yourself! To do this, first mix all the wet ingredients together with great vigor. So eggs, flour, water and so on. Then you stir the finely chopped cabbage into this mass. And then everything else, for example, the fish or meat provided.

On the table you will usually find oil (put some of it on the teppan), okonomiyaki sauce (put a lot of it on the finished patty, just before eating it) and mayonnaise (put even more of it on the finished patty, nicely crossed and sweeping), and then the finished patty will look perfect. There you have it, your first homemade okonomiyaki! If necessary, just watch the people sitting next to you while they enjoy their first beer and see how they prepare their dishes. Watching your neighbor is also the best way to gauge the perfect height (very thick!) of the finished dish. Again, okonomiyaki has nothing to do with pancakes or crepes, and thus should be more than an inch tall, after which its interior will be perfectly creamy.

So here we have okonomiyaki, which is prepared on the teppan. With that, you now know two important words in Japanese cuisine: yaki means to grill, pan fry or otherwise cook on direct heat, and teppan is the proper name for the flat, stainless steel cooking surface at American "hibachi" restaurants. Both words together describe another delicious way to eat in Japan: Teppanyaki.

In a ***teppanyaki*** restaurant, too, skillets are embedded in the counter and a chef will prepare all dishes freshly in front of the customers. Places with the same setup, but skillets installed in the tables are called yakiniku restaurants, a word that obviously consists of "yaki" again, complemented by the word "niku" for meat. Mostly, the guests grill themselves here, and thanks to very effective ventilation technology, the air extraction in these restaurants is usually so good that you can step back onto the street completely odorless despite a grilling adventure lasting several hours. This is ensured by high-performance fans hidden next to the grill surface, and additionally by large exhaust vents above the tables. During the COVID-19 pandemic, yakiniku restaurants were considered the safest places in Japan because a high volume of air is quickly and constantly extracted at each table and expelled outside.

The food in and of itself can be just about anything you can grill, not only meat but also many varieties of fish and veggies. The ingredients are served in bite-sized portions, so that you can easily eat with chopsticks. If pieces of meat are larger, a pair of kitchen shears is always available - which is very unusual the first time, but in Japan kitchen shears are as much a part of grilling as barbecue tongs and oversized spatulas are in the States. With the help of the shears, steaks, cutlets and all other large pieces of meat are cut into small pieces that conform to the chopstick.

In the upscale teppanyaki restaurants where a chef prepares the food course by course in front of the guests, the ingredients can become pretty exceptional. They don't serve pork chops or meatballs, but rather duck liver, a whole lobster or a perfect piece of wagyu steak.

Speaking of ***wagyu***, this meat is so legendary that I would like to go a little deeper into it.

In the USA, wagyu is often marketed as Kobe beef, which doesn't quite hit the nail on the head. For the genus of cattle called wagyu, it consists of several different breeds and is by no means only bred in the city of Kobe. It was only from there that the first wagyu meat came to the United States.

According to various Japanese chefs I have spoken to about this, the best wagyu does not always come from the Kobe region either. And, you guessed it, according to these chefs, the quality of the meat varies every season anyway depending on the weather, the resulting quality of grass in different areas of Japan, and basically the exact date of slaughter. Was it too warm on the days before slaughter, was the cattle stressed, was the cattle too cold, did they eat too little in the last few days and thus not have the optimal fat structure? Talking about food is always a highly developed science in Japan.

Back to the Wagyu meat itself. What makes this meat special is the very noticeable marbling of its fat. There is not "meat here, fat edge there", but an evenly marbled and very beautiful piece of "meat with continuous fat graining". Red and white, harmoniously distributed.

What many people don't consider is that this means that each and every bite of this meat is very fatty. Delicious, but fatty. Wagyu should therefore be eaten in small portions to really be enjoyed, otherwise it will be as heavy in your stomach as a pound of butter.

I would say that four adults can enjoyably share a classic wagyu steak. It's cooked to perfection, then cut into bite-sized pieces and eaten. Or you can grill a few wafer-thin wagyu slices yourself, which can be bought pre-cut in Japan at the butcher and at many supermarket meat counters.

These consumption quantities should be kept in mind before ordering a huge piece of Wagyu all by yourself for a hundred dollars and more. There are fast diminishing returns to the joy of eating wagyu once you reach a certain quantity, so save yourself from stomach problems later in the evening and enjoy fatty beef in moderation!

Now that we've explored the word “yaki” in several ways already, let's move on to the **yakitori restaurant**. So, as we discussed previously, yaki means grilled. What might “tori” mean? Its actually “bird”! In the case of many food names, like now, tori is used to mean chicken. But please don't think that yakitori is about half or whole chickens being rotated and roasted by the hundreds in stainless steel racks around a gas grill. Yakitori has as much in common with rotisserie chicken as a bag of grape juice has with a vintage champagne.

For yakitori, the guest orders and pays for individual skewers of grilled food. You need a few of these to get your fill. Be warned: The costs add up quickly here.

The vast majority of skewers consist of pure chicken pieces. There are significantly more pieces that can be cut from such a chicken than the common fried chicken connoisseur would dream of: outer breast, inner breast, minced breast meat, liver, upper leg, lower leg, rump, neck, ovaries, stomach, heart, skin and finally - cartilage. Personally, I really dislike the texture of all the abovementioned offal. But you can't go wrong with breast and leg in different variations.

A yakitori restaurant is often a very cozy and a very delicious place. Sitting at the bar, drinking a few beers and eating a never-ending stream of freshly grilled skewers is a perfect and very popular way to end the day in Japan.

Of course, if you want to take it to the extreme, you can try one of the Michelin-starred yakitoris and be served what are probably the juiciest, crispiest, and most delicious chicken pieces of your life. On my visit to one of these temples of chicken, our taste experience was further crowned by what was rumored to be a hundred-year-old sauce that was used to coat many of the skewers. Where, of course, ingredients are replenished daily. But the chef reported with polite pride that his clay pot had never been completely emptied since 1920 and had never been cleaned.

After all these not-so-easy-to-cook-at-home dishes, we now turn to home cooking. Let's move on to the pork cutlet. Known as schnitzel in Germany, in Japan it's called **tonkatsu** and is extremely crispy, breaded with panko, a particularly flaky Japanese breadcrumb. Tonkatsu is sold by the hundreds of thousands in supermarkets, fast-food restaurants, konbinis, canteens and, of course, in dedicated tonkatsu restaurants. Tonkatsu is always made with pork (the "ton" in the name refers to pork) and actually always delicious. In fact, I can't remember having a single bad tonkatsu.

It is usually eaten with a dark gravy and rice. When it is on a bowl of rice ("don"), it is called "katsudon" and I recommend this dish without reservation. Tonkatsu always goes down well and somehow makes you happy.

Even more common than tonkatsu is **curry**. And that, in turn, is something like the secret star of Japanese cuisine. Outside Japan, Japanese curry is hard to come by, but in the island kingdom it's a hit. Freeway service stations, school canteens, snack bars - they all serve curry. But a Japanese curry is not yellow, but rather brown. It's based on a thick sauce, which is usually only slightly spicy. In addition, there are some small pieces of meat, rarely some greens, but always some chunks of vegetables in the gravy, with pickled vegetables served on the side, without exception. Combined with a large portion of rice, resulting in a Japanese national dish that is quite unknown in the West.

Of course, there is also fancy Japanese curry, for example in small, fine curry restaurants, where various sauces are freshly cooked every day from any number of exotic spices. But in most cases, the Japanese eat curry as a commercial or home kitchen product. Whereby it must be said that a large pot does not seem to harm the quality of a curry. As with tonkatsu, I have never eaten a curry that didn't taste good. It's usually very inexpensive, it fills you up, it's delicious - a bit like good goulash with a hint of hot peppers. Who doesn't like that?

In Japanese supermarkets, there are often long aisles stocked with curry concentrates for the home. Next to rice, these curry concentrates are the country's best-selling category of goods, from countless manufacturers and often offered in three, five or even seven different degrees of spiciness. From extra sweet children's curry to fiery hot devil's curry - every manufacturer has a wide range on offer.

But as I said, in the vast majority of restaurants curry is only a slightly spicy affair and can be recommended without reservation. Here I must mention that my colleague Niharika, who comes from India, regularly told me that the very saucy Japanese curry was a unique invention and in no way deserved the name "curry". To her, everything was missing here - spiciness, the right spices, meat and vegetables. So if you're a big fan of authentic Indian cuisine, you might want to steer clear of the Japonized version of this dish.

I will discuss various typical snacks in Japan in detail in the chapter on the small convenience stores or konbinis. Therefore, I'll skip delicious snacks like onigiri and fine sweets like mochi and go straight to the supreme discipline of Japanese cuisine. The gastronomic highlight of an authentic trip to Japan. The feast that can be perfectly documented in photos: **a kaiseki menu**.

The easiest way to get a kaiseki meal is to book an overnight stay at a ryokan. With very few exceptions, the food there is an integral part of the booking - and incidentally also the biggest price driver. But of course you can also enjoy kaiseki in restaurants, at least most of the time. There are also kaiseki restaurants that only accept new guests on the recommendation of previous guests. There are several reasons for this. One of them is to make sure that no horde of barbaric foreigners loudly attacks the holiest of holies of Japanese cuisine ... But with a little luck, Japanese acquaintances, a good hotel concierge or specialized websites can often get you a table here. So just try, and if it works, be sure to behave yourself!

So what is this kaiseki? It is a comprehensive art form of food preparation. In no other meal is so much emphasis placed on balance, beauty, perfect flavor, local and seasonal ingredients, and craftsmanship. Attention is paid not only to the ingredients and their preparation, but also to the shape, color and materiality of each plate, bowl and glass. Everything must fit together; everything must complement each other.

Kaiseki cuisine had a massive influence on the so-called "nouvelle cuisine" in Europe and the US, and the trends that are now fashionable in the West, such as maximum seasonality and consistent use of local ingredients, were already practiced at Kaiseki in the ninth century AD. Often referred to as the "world's best" restaurant in the 2010s, "Noma" was also famous, among other things, for using the kaiseki principle of individual, hand-crafted plates for each dish.

Today's kaiseki cuisine reflects four schools of Japanese cuisine. The imperial cuisine, developed in the ninth century, the Buddhist, vegetarian temple cuisine of the twelfth century, the sophisticated samurai cuisine of the fourteenth century, and finally, the particularly light tea ceremony cuisine of the fifteenth century. Each of these schools set a different emphasis, and each chef mixes the traditions a little differently today. With a little effort, however, you can find the pure, traditional schools of cuisine. The easiest way to do this is with the Buddhist vegetarian tradition. This is especially strong in the Kyoto area, but also in the many monasteries that accept overnight guests.

In my favorite Kaiseki restaurant, the menu changed fifty-two times a year. Each week had its specialties. And always according to the ingredients that had the absolute perfect quality somewhere in Japan in that exact week.

Here, dish after dish was served with great kindness and absolute perfection. In a room made entirely of cedar, with a frameless window overlooking the garden, where you could admire an ancient plum tree. Each component of the meal was served on different china or earthenware, depending on what the chef thought was the most visually harmonious combination. Even the alternating sake with the different courses was served in a different decanter and with different cups each time made of clay, metal or wood. Always chosen to ensure both the character of the sake and harmony with the other bowls of the current course on the table.

Over the course of a good kaiseki meal, you eat many different vegetables, sashimi, something cooked, something fried, soup, rice and something sweet. Marinated, fermented, seasoned, raw or in a mix of different ways of preparation. Spread over ten to twenty courses, each with a wide variety of small plates and bowls. It is a herculean effort.

And as I said, the eye always eats with you. You really have to take the time to look at each dish and let it sink in. And you should ask your waiter questions - in English or with Google Translate. Eating is only really fun when you understand exactly what you have in front of you, why it's on the menu this week, how and why it was prepared exactly the way it was, and how you should eat it.

Due to the very high regionality of Kaiseki cuisine, you will find a lot of fish and seafood in a Kaiseki menu near the sea. Inland, on the other hand, you will often find game or beef. And as I said, in the Buddhist-oriented restaurants all over the country, vegetarians can also easily and very deeply immerse themselves in the Japanese art of cooking - which is otherwise very difficult.

Restaurant Guide from the High Mass of Culinary Art to Alcohol Flat Rate

Hidden, secret restaurants are not exactly rare in Japan. They are called ryotei and often housed in old villas, indistinguishable from the outside from other large private residences. There are no signs, no bell, sometimes no phone number or email address to contact them. You can only get into these restaurants through personal recommendations with the owner, who will then put you on the guest list if necessary. And that in turn creates so much exclusivity and thus hype that this business model works quite excellently.

My first Ryotei experience was a completely random stroke of luck. One evening in spring, my friend Peter and I stood hungry and thirsty in front of the closed door of a restaurant that a Japanese friend had recommended to us as an insider tip. But neither shaking nor disbelieving knocking helped us that evening - the door was locked. Perplexed, we checked our cell phones for alternatives. And surprisingly, we were shown an excellently rated restaurant on the other side of the street. However, there was nothing to be seen there. Two garages, an old house covered with rusty corrugated iron, a small bakery. Google, however, reported a tempura restaurant right there. We searched the whole street for a sign or an entrance to this restaurant in vain. Just as we were about to call a cab to try our luck elsewhere, a small door in the corrugated metal facade opened, and a well-dressed couple stumbled out onto the street, slightly tipsy, to go on their way. Surely this had to be our restaurant...? A little unsure whether we were about to find ourselves in a secret poker club, we opened the door, and there we were, standing in a very tasteful, very Japanese restaurant with eight seats and a Michelin star on the checkroom wall. We had indeed found the restaurant. And for the next two and a half hours, we sank into a work of art of Japanese craftsmanship, culinary art, and hospitality.

After this discovery, I specifically searched for other hidden restaurants among my acquaintances. I had my best Ryotei experience a few months later in an old villa, which was located in a private park in the middle of a residential area in Setagaya. Our Japanese friend Misaki had recommended us to the owner there and also vouched for us. So one evening we stood in front of the large wooden gate of this property and pushed the latch aside, slightly nervously. The gate opened onto a wide staircase that disappeared in a left turn between fragrant jasmine bushes. A butler was waiting there to greet us in three languages. Japanese, English and even German! We had never experienced that before. In an incredibly friendly manner, he accompanied us to the house.

The old Japanese villa had been built a hundred years ago and then recently renovated by the current owner, an interior and retail designer. All visible elements of the house were either gray stone or cement, light Japanese cedar or midnight black iron. Greatly reduced, very Japanese and very impressive. Clearly, the kaiseki experience here did not begin with the first course, but with the premises.

We were led into a room that housed only two tables and a counter facing the kitchen, and a single, large window in one of the walls. Again, the only materials used were wood, metal and stone. Since the room was so quiet and austere except for that large window, patrons instinctively gazed through the window. Its cutout in the wall was so perfectly chosen that the Japanese garden behind it appeared like a brightly shining painting.

Throughout the meal, where each course was served in beautiful handmade bowls and dishes, you really felt like you were taking part in a spiritual event. Simply because everything was so perfectly harmonious. Not kitschy, not luxurious, not over the top - just perfect. When we left the restaurant again after a good two hours, we walked the five kilometers home - for once we didn't feel like taking the subway, we wanted to take a little bit of that peaceful atmosphere with us.

Of course, it's not just the top-end restaurants that enchant. As written elsewhere, there is nothing that does not exist here. But if you're going to make the long trip, I would always try to visit at least one of these very special and very high-end restaurants. It's simply an experience you can't get anywhere else in the world.

Here's a tip to help manage your wallet while eating your heart out all over Japan: Nomihodai. This is the magic word for a lot of fun on a small budget in Japanese restaurants and izakayas and means “all you can drink”. Nomihodai is often supplemented by a predefined menu of dishes, sometimes even in the "all you can eat" variant, which is called tabehodai. While normal à la carte eating and drinking in Japan is rather expensive and a heavy burden on many travelers' budgets, nomihodai reverses this completely. It is always extremely cheap in relation, often costing only between two thousand and three thousand yen, or around twenty dollars. In return, all the drinks on a special nomihodai menu are free-flowing. In most cases, this includes draft beer, wine, sparkling wine, sake, mixed drinks and soft drinks. You can't ask for more than that. As a rule, the offer is valid for two hours, with "last order" after ninety minutes. At this point, the professional orders another three drinks to make good use of the remaining half hour - Japanese modesty is no longer expected of anyone present after an hour and a half of drinking. Accordingly, all orders of the "last order" are served without complaint, so that one sits at the end of his compact two-hour binge in front of very many empty glasses, has eaten deliciously and staggers rather full, happy and drunk to the train. Together with thousands of other nomihodai consumers of this evening.

In many restaurants, nomihodai must be reserved a day in advance. The reason for this is to serve nomikai (after hours or after work drinking) groups and planned celebrations among friends, rather than spontaneous couples or tourists looking to pay lower prices. However, if the latter have made a reservation the day before, they are served just as well as everyone else.

In recent years, "grill-yourself" nomihodai deals have also become popular, where you book a two-hour free-flow of drinks, a gas grill and an assortment of fish, meat and vegetables in a garden, on a terrace or, at best, on a rooftop. Even very expensive bars and restaurants in the city center offer such deals, at least on weekdays and earlier evenings. We once had a barbecue this way on the fiftieth floor of a high rise, high above Shibuya Crossing on a super exclusive rooftop terrace overlooking all of Tokyo, and got terribly drunk with good friends from the neighborhood. Which was also due to the fact that you got both beer and whiskey highballs in three-liter containers to tap yourself on the table on request. Normally, you paid eight euros for a single glass of highball up here. In the context of our nomihodai, it was available by the liter, plus really delicious food, for less than thirty bucks per person.

Of baguette, baumkuchen and hammered rice porridge

Japan likes its sweets. Not sticky sweets like some pastries in the Orient, but sugar can be found not only in cakes, but consistently in white bread and, for some unknown reason, likewise in most pizzas. Traditionally, dessert is not as much of a focus as in the West, but the appetite for Western sweet treats is high. And so Tokyo is littered with bakeries, mostly with French and sometimes Scandinavian names, that supply the population with pastries and all kinds of starch and sugar dishes.

The traditional Japanese candy stores - namagashi stores – take a bit of a back seat. There, they mainly sell variations of mochi, which are small rice flour cakes or dumplings, often with a red bean filling. Mochi have recently become somewhat better known in the West, especially in the form of ice cream with a mochi dough coating. In Japan, mochi are about half the size of a tennis ball and come in a variety of colors and flavors. They don't taste too sweet, but there is actually a lot of sugar in these delicious morsels.

Traditionally, the production of mochi is a lot of work. You put freshly cooked rice into a large wooden bowl and then beat the rice with two large wooden hammers into a fine paste. This requires two strong people to steadily pound the rice and often another helper to stir the rice mixture at the same time. Such freshly prepared mochi is very fluffy and really yummy.

The easier way to get good results as well, besides large-scale industrial production, is to make your own mochi paste at home using rice flour, water and a microwave. Instructions for this are plentiful on the Internet, if you want to try your luck.

In addition to mochi paste, which is essentially rice flour or the hammered rice just described, red bean paste, or anko, has an equally large influence on Japanese sweets. It comes along not only as a filling for mochi, but for almost anything that is somehow soft and sweet-tasting. Milk roll? Gladly with anko filling.

Pancakes? In Japan, they almost always have an anko core. Vanilla ice cream? Tastes better with a spoonful of anko dolloped on top.

The beans used to make anko are called azuki beans, and you can get them everywhere in Japan. I thought for a long time that they were very sweet by nature, until I made paste from them myself for the first time - the mixing ratio with sugar is one to one. This is also the reason why filled mochi and the like are not as low in calories as they might seem.

However, my favorite Japanese dessert is taiyaki. These are about ten centimeters in size, baked fish from a pancake batter in the shape of sea bream. Very pretty to look at. These little pancake fish are filled with custard or, traditionally, with anko. At fairs and temple festivals taiyaki are often grilled fresh using large cast-iron molds that sit steaming over the coals. Anko is then inserted between two of these fish-shaped pancakes, wich are then folded atop each other and served hot. The easier-to-get version is shrink-wrapped and waiting for hungry customers in the refrigerator section of the nearest konbini. Here, the pancake fish are not as diverse in texture: no crispy edges and no fluffy pancake interior, but rather a consistently rubbery texture. But well, the store-bought taiyaki still taste quite excellent.

In addition, there are of course many other desserts, such as various jellies based on agar. But all the different variations of mochi and anko alone, cover a surprisingly large part of traditional Japanese sweet cuisine. Perhaps another reason why Western bakeries are so popular –is because they are simply more diverse.

I have already written that you can find better baguettes and croissants in Tokyo than in most parts of Europe and even better than in many French bakeries. The unconditional pursuit of perfection of Japanese bakers pays off here for the hungry customer. Confectionery quality is also very high, but the selection here is often much more adapted to local Japanese tastes and therefore more surprising. What you can find everywhere, for example, is pastries with matcha, the famous green tea powder. Green buns, green cakes, green creams and green muffins are standard. If you like matcha, it tastes great, but can be unfamiliar.

Then there are a lot of pastries with chestnut filling and using chestnuts in general. Mont Blanc, the French dessert made of chestnut paste and cream, is a kind of national dish in Japan - you can get mont blanc tarts in every bakery and mont blanc cream in every konbini. There are also pieces of chestnut in Danish pastries, chestnuts in buns and a kind of dough ball with a large chestnut in the middle.

By the way, a specialty of sweets in Japan is a very German pastry: - log cakes! It's known by its German name here: Baumkuchen. It began its life in Japan shortly after the First World War in the bakery of the German confectioner Karl Juchheim in Yokohama. It is today a nationally enjoyed dish, in fact far more so than in Germany. Why baumkuchen became so successful is a matter of speculation. One positive is that it keeps for several days even in hot, humid climates, which is an invaluable advantage in the Japanese summer. Also, it has a pleasant consistency, not too firm, not too soft. And it has a subtle flavor that you have to chase a bit. All of these aspects are things that meet Japanese preferences well. Perhaps it was then additionally the pretty shape or the decorative rings of the cake that contributed to its success. In any case, today it is impossible to imagine Japanese confectionery without it. And since hardly any bakers in Germany still make baumkuchen by hand, a vacation in Japan offers a great opportunity for Germans to taste a very traditional German cake, handmade and freshly baked, at least once in their life.

Another Japanese national dish, which is rather unknown as such, is strawberry tart. Very classically prepared with a sponge cake base, cream and lots of fresh strawberries, this is not a summer specialty or a spring custom. On the contrary, strawberry tart is a classic gift and also a family dessert on Christmas in Japan. Our Japanese friends were completely perplexed when we told them that no one in our country eats strawberry cake on Christmas. For them, it was as much a part of Christmas as the festively decorated trees in the department stores.

The background here is that Christmas in Japan is not a Christian tradition but was established as a celebration of love under the American occupation after World War II. Therefore, on Christmas Eve, many people eat a nice meal with their family, while others meet their date (married or otherwise), visit a good restaurant and polish off large amounts of red and white strawberry cake, which apparently reminds people of innocence and love.

According to reports, the birth rate in Japan is at its highest every year at the end of September, nine months after Christmas. Strawberry cake has therefore also been proven to have an aphrodisiac effect in the land of the rising sun.

The wonder world of Japanese supermarkets and konbinis

A Japanese supermarket is basically structured in the same way as a supermarket in the West. With the big difference is that you won't be familiar with many of the products except some big brands like Coca-Cola. Even most of the vegetables are exotic; only broccoli and spring onions are always available everywhere. Easier to understand are the food courts in the basements of large supermarkets and department stores. This is because ready-made food is offered here, making it easier for the slightly overwhelmed visitor to imagine what he or she is about to eat. Especially in the department stores, where they are used to international customers, you can order and buy most things with a little bit of English and hand gestures, even without any knowledge of Japanese.

Even easier to use than food courts are the countless small konbinis. The name is derived from "convenience store", and I have already used it frequently in the previous chapters. It is a kind of mixture between a kiosk and a gas station, only without gas pumps. Here you can find everything you need to live in a small space. The best-known chains are Lawson, Family Mart and 7-Eleven. The original American 7-Eleven chain also exists in many other countries around the world, but the level of stores in Japan cannot be compared to any other country and is especially miles away from the quality of the unkempt American branches. (Fun fact: The Japanese licensee of the 7-Eleven brand became so successful that they bought the American 7-Eleven parent company! 7-Eleven is now a global brand, based in Japan, and the US operation is just a subsidiary.) Once again, Japan has first introduced a concept from abroad, then analyzed and optimized it to a much higher level.

What can you buy or do now in such a konbini? I'll try to write a small instruction manual so that my readers can at least bring a delicious meal and some drinks from the konbini to their hotel room on their very first day in Japan, when they are still a bit afraid of the ramen restaurants and shy of the izakayas. Before sleeping off the jet lag there.

When you enter the Konbini, the two or three employees almost always call out a joyful "*Irasshaimaseee*" to you. This means "welcome" and does not have to be answered. However, a friendly "*Konnichiwa*" can never hurt.

In the first aisle next to the entrance, you will then usually find drugstore items. So, for example, sunscreen or lip cream, but also practical disposable heat pads in winter or disposable cooling pads in summer. In addition, there are always umbrellas, at least until the rain starts. After half an hour of downpour, the stock is often sold out. In some konbinis you can also find the most important basics to wear. Socks and shirts, for example, packed in tiny compact packages, but of surprisingly robust quality.

Somewhere, preferably near the first aisle, there is always a small refrigerated shelf with magic juices. At the top are energy drinks like Red Bull and lots of Japanese variants of the same. Some of them are really very strong, so you should be a bit more careful.

In addition, on this shelf you can find a lot of vitamin juices. Very tasty, for example, is a vitamin C preparation from Pokka Sapporo in a green bottle with a white label showing a lemon and a green cross. It's great for refreshment and wakes you up - and with a little potato schnapps, you can even make a very formidable Vodka Lemon out of it. Other vitamin preparations on the shelf come in brown bottles, look more like medicine and taste like old cough syrup. I wouldn't bother with those.

An absolute highlight of these small refrigerated shelves are the anti-hangover drinks. Every salaryman and also many a colleague from my company drink these before and after going out in the evening. The main ingredient of these drinks in small metal bottles with screw tops is turmeric, or yellow ginger. The taste of the concoction is horrible, and the thick consistency is not for me at all. But I can confirm that one bottle before and, depending on the course of the evening, one to three bottles after the binge will help avoid just about any hangover.

However, the fact that no Western start-up has yet jumped into mass production for the non-Japanese market leads me to suspect that there may be other ingredients besides turmeric that are not sanctioned medicinally around the world. But anyway, the vials work wonders.

The most famous of these anti-hangover remedies is called "Ukon No Chikara" or “The Strength of Turmeric”. It comes in small golden metal bottles and features a bright little ginger root on the label. It's hard to miss. Harder variants of hangover preventatives contain beef liver extract, and instead of the little glowing roots, they show glowing livers. It looks so gruesome that I never bought this stuff – neither sober nor after several bottles of sake.

Back to the layout of our konbini. After the magic refrigerated shelf, there are now two to three aisles with somewhat more ordinary contents, like everything from coffee to sweets and salty treats to any number of beverages. Here, the oversized tetrapaks with up to three liters of sake or even high-proof shochu schnapps stand out most clearly. In Japan, you can get very drunk for very cheap if necessary, which certainly also explains the statistically significant increase in the number of alcoholics in the country in recent years.

On the wall opposite the entrance, there is pure konbini magic again: meters of refrigerated shelves with prepared food, and almost all of it tastes really good! From spaghetti bolognese to all kinds of salads, rice dishes, schnitzel, fish, mapo tofu and soba dishes to various kinds of ramen, sushi, sashimi, hamburgers and sandwiches. As for the sandwiches, many people swear by the egg salad versions, but personally I didn't find them mind-blowing. Very nice to look at and unusual are the sandwiches with cream and strawberries available from January to about April. Eating such a sandwich is as filling as polishing off a large slice of Black Forest cake.

In addition to all of the above dishes, there is always a shelf of onigiri, the famous Japanese rice triangles. Think of it as a good handful of fat, sticky Japanese rice shaped into a triangle, often with a filling such as tuna and mayonnaise or salty plum (honestly, these are extremely salty). Onigiri are classically formed by hand in the morning in many homes, wrapped in a narrow sheet of nori seaweed and taken to school or work as a snack.

The problem: The nori leaf, which is nice and crispy in itself, becomes soft when left wrapped around the wet rice for some time. Therefore, many Japanese wrap their rice in the sheet just before eating. Of course, this would be a bit inconvenient with food from the supermarket and also unhygienic. Therefore, an ingenious wrapping has been developed in Japan, which I find difficult to describe in words: A triangular foil package wraps around the small rice triangle, its corners labeled one, two, and three. By pulling on tab one, you open the package in the middle, as if you were opening a zipper. By carefully pulling on corner number two, one now removes one half of the outer wrapper, but at the same time one also removes a connected inner wrapper, which additionally lay between the rice triangle and the surrounding nori sheet. If one presses a little on the just freed nori sheet at the free lying rice part, the seaweed sticks directly to the rice and remains there.

Now pull off corner number three as well, thus removing the plastic film between the seaweed and the rice on the other side as well, and repeat its careful application to the rice. Et voilà: You now hold a perfect triangle of rice wrapped in fresh, crispy nori. Thanks to the seaweed leaf, it not only looks beautiful, but nori and rice also taste great together. And, big bonus: your fingers won't stick to the rice. Bravo!

We now continue towards the checkout counter. There are usually a few more great features waiting there. For example, there is the warming counter with deep-fried chicken breast pieces in various flavors. Legendary are the chicken nuggets at Lawson's, which are freshly prepared in every Lawson's konbini and regularly win fast food competitions.

There are also corn dogs at the warming counter! These are very thick hot dog sausages breaded in corn dough, deep fried and served on a wooden stick. Experiments I have conducted have shown that a single corn dog can easily satiate a full-grown person for half a day.

Behind the checkout counter, and sometimes next to it for self-service, are large and very powerful microwaves. These are there to heat up the food just selected in the refrigerated section in just a few seconds. The store employees will usually ask you if you want the food hot ("Obento atatamemasuka?"). Here, you simply answer "Hai!" and they put the chosen dish in the microwave for you.

If there are self-service microwaves, each dish has printed on it how many minutes and seconds it should be reheated at how many watts. These times are easy to read. "2分30秒" means 2 minutes and 30 seconds, and especially the kanji for minute 分 is easy to see. However, what is very important is that two different heating times are usually given. For a microwave at home, with about 500 watts. And for the professional microwave in the konbini, with a good 1500 watts. I didn't know that at the beginning of my time in Japan, and managed to explode a whole bowl of ramen noodles in a very powerful konbini microwave....

Next to the microwaves, many konbinis have a good coffee machine. After the rapid advance of Starbucks, these were introduced nationwide by the konbini chains a few years ago and now supply the whole country with delicious coffee from one hundred yen, which is less than one dollar for the cup. Most of the time, you buy the appropriate cup at the counter and then draw your own fresh coffee with it. Thanks to an illustrated menu with all the available drinks, this is a very simple exercise, and the quality of the coffee is really excellent considering its price.

In addition to all the products described and thousands of other items, you can also take advantage of various services at konbini. You can certainly buy stamps here, as is to be expected, but these small supermarkets also have ticket machines for just about everything Japan's stages have to offer - from tickets for the upcoming Rolling Stones tour to traditional kabuki theater to tickets for aquariums. However, you can't switch the language of these vending machines to English. For tourists, therefore, they are almost impossible to use.

What everyone can use, however, are the free toilets in many konbini. These are a dream come true, especially with small children, as it feels like there is a place to wash your hands every few hundred meters in Japanese cities. It is also very practical to always know where you can find clean toilets and sinks.

Every konbini also has an ATM. Especially at 7-Eleven, international bank and credit cards work much more reliably here than at most banks. 7-Eleven actually runs its own bank in Japan with good facilities for foreign account holders, and their konbini ATMs have good English menus to help facilitate international remittances.

Bank ATMs, on the other hand, are a different story. ATMs at banks have working hours for some inexplicable reason. As a rule, these adorable machines celebrate closing time from 10:00pm at the latest. Only the machines in the konbinis distribute cash around the clock.

As a resident of Japan, you don't just withdraw money at konbini, you also pay bills there. That's because the Japanese don't pay many of their bills by bank transfer, but in cash at the nearest convenience store. Electricity, gas, Amazon orders or parking tickets - in Japan, all these bills come with a barcode that can be scanned by the konbini cash register. And because bank transfers are complicated, inconvenient and expensive in Japan, this direct payment service at the supermarket checkout is used extensively.

Another feature of the Konbini is that there is always a copier and fax machine there. During the first COVID-19 lockdown, many of my colleagues made a daily pilgrimage to the nearest konbini to print out documents. That saves some space at home, plus the konbini never runs out of ink or paper.

One last function of the konbinis is worth mentioning: they also act as important, decentralized supply helpers in the event of severe earthquakes. Thanks to the excellent logistics networks of their operators, their huge stockpiles throughout Japan and the relatively safe construction of most konbinis consisting of single-story concrete buildings with surrounding parking lots, they provide valuable support for surrounding populations in the event of a disaster. Accordingly, many konbinis are also equipped with emergency generators, and their operators work closely with regional disaster management authorities.

Family and Friendship in Japan

Super mom and salaryman - the complicated gender roles in Japan

The relationship between men and women in Japan is difficult and opaque. In a strange and paradoxical way, hardcore machismo meets authoritarian matriarchy.

Formally speaking, Japan is an almost backward country when it comes to equal rights for men and women. The World Economic Forum determines a Global Gender Gap every year. 1.0 is the best possible result, meaning there are virtually no differences between the treatment of the sexes. Iceland achieved a top score of 0.91 in 2023, and the US came in at 0.75, while Japan was far off with 0.65, close to Jordan and India. To its credit, however, all of East Asia seems to have a problem here. China and South Korea also score close to the Empire of the Rising Sun.

It is remarkable that in Japan gender inequality is not reflected in schools nor in universities - in fact, a markedly large number of women study through the university level in Japan. However, a great many of these young women disappear from the workforce when their first child is born and don't come back.

This is a combination of various phenomena that are very difficult for outsiders to comprehend and can hardly be recognized when reading statistics. For example, some female students have no intention of working for very long after completing their studies. With plenty of pressure from their parents, they simply study anything at a less prestigious university without any goal of finding professional fulfillment or achieving higher academic degrees. Instead, they study pragmatically because a university degree makes them much more attractive on the marriage market than not. And the marriage market in Japan is very, very classical, to say the least.

To this day, there are many marriages that are completely arranged by parents, grandparents or other relatives. Especially when the children and grandchildren complete their education and are not yet involved with a special someone, the family becomes nervous and sometimes becomes very active in changing this.

In the past, young Japanese women liked to be called "Christmas Cake". Very attractive up to their twenty-fourth birthday, but no one wants them after the twenty-fifth. Today, however, the image has changed to "New Years Cake" and thirty-one is considered the new critical threshold for getting hitched.

Occasionally published statistics of Japanese dating portals show that female profiles with university degrees are by far the most clicked. With the greatest attractiveness up to the age of twenty-five and a very sharp drop at thirty-one. Male profiles must also include a university degree, but the protagonists may quietly be several years older and are not considered unattractive until around forty years of age.

Young people are obviously under a lot of pressure to bring a well-off and educated spouse into the house. This may read like a bad novel from the last century, but love is often just one component among many in Japan when it comes to finding the right partner.

Of course, there are also a huge number of ambitious and very successful female students, especially at the country's extremely selective top universities such as Tokyo University or Waseda University. Anyone who earns a diploma from one of these universities can virtually choose their employer at will.

But even among these graduates, it is reportedly very common for highly talented women with great educations to drop out of the workforce after the birth of their first child. What is the reason for this?

First of all, it should be noted that Japanese society does not particularly appreciate working mothers. The general attitude of the masses towards mothers is that they should take care of the little Japanese around the clock.

There is generous maternal and even parental (for both mom and dad) support available, but the reality is not as nice as the basic rules read... Women (as well as men!) can choose to take off up to one paid year for taking care of their newborn children. Due to losing the important bonus (30-40% of the annual salary) and still having to pay most taxes, the 50-66% payout rate of the last income before giving birth results in a much more severe drop in income than it looks like on paper. In addition, daycare is very hard to come by. The low availability of daycare centers causing mothers to lose their jobs because they are stuck on wait lists for daycare for more than three years and thus lose their return to job guarantee. And what about that parental leave for fathers? Well... only low single digits of Japanese men make ever use of this. In a culture where peer pressure already makes you refrain from taking holidays, taking parental leave is pretty unthinkable for most men.

Various friends in Japan have reported to me that pressure is often exerted on the current generation of young mothers by their mothers-in-law, who themselves stayed at home in the 1970s and 1980s, to please take leave from their jobs. Time and again, we also hear that male colleagues make disparaging remarks about pregnant female colleagues or young mothers because they are less flexible in working overtime and thus supposedly shift their own work onto the group of colleagues.

And so, unfortunately, it still happens far too often today that Japanese women pull the ripcord and quit because of the incompatibility of social demands, family pressure and their demanding jobs.

The frequent drop-out of top female academics from the job market caused a scandal at the renowned Tokyo Medical University in 2018. A newspaper revealed that female applicants for a place on a medical course there had been rated ten to twenty percent lower than male applicants by the examination board over a period of years. The petty justification of the convicted professors: Women would only work in hospitals and medical practices for a few years after their demanding studies and then retire from professional life. Therefore, they would rather use the valuable university resources for male students.

I think it speaks volumes that, in the face of this situation, the (exclusively male) examiners did not launch an initiative to make the profession of medicine compatible with child rearing, but simply consistently thwarted women.

However, it is not only the expectations of parents and in-laws that push women to withdraw from their careers. The seemingly endless unwritten rules on how to integrate and engage with children in Japanese society have a much stronger effect.

Men are largely excluded from this. After all, they have to work (meaning work consistently long hours of overtime during the week and often weekends). So the woman shoulders a large part of the obligatory (not voluntary!) parental time commitments at elementary school, in at daycare and preschool, in the sports club, in the community and in the neighborhood, to name just a few.

I will try to illustrate this with an example. Using my friend Ayumi, whose mother and grandmother have always worked as retailers, and who herself cannot imagine not working anymore.

Ayumi is thirty-three years old, a full-time professional, a mother of a daughter in kindergarten and a son in elementary school: every morning she gets up at 4:30 a.m. and prepares bento boxes for her children. Why does she do it by hand? Because all the other moms in kindergarten and school do it too. And her children have tearfully reported how the teachers criticized them for their supermarket-bought bentos in the past. Since then, Ayumi has been cooking every morning.

Her husband at least made sure that both children were awake and dressed, and After cooking and changing the kids she takes the son to the bus. This morning Ayumi is on duty for the kindergarten. Twenty mothers have been assigned to it. Wearing a yellow vest, she stands at a crosswalk for half an hour. The other mothers guard nineteen other crosswalks and pedestrian lights. With a yellow flag in their hands, they don't slow down cars, but just watch over the children. They are not supposed to disturb the flow of traffic, so Ayumi holds her flag in front of a group of children and waits until the road clears. Then she raises her flag, and the children are allowed to go. Since it is in a residential area, only four or five cars pass by in the half hour. And the children would probably wait dutifully until the cars pass, even without Ayumi. In any case, duty is duty.

After that she goes to the office and works until 12:00. She has taken the afternoon off, because it is meeting of the school newspaper. At the beginning of the school year, the honorary offices were distributed among the mothers of the class. There is not a single honorary office that would be filled by a man. Ayumi had trembled and sweated that the chalice of an elaborate honorary office might pass her by. But she was unlucky and was appointed to be in charge of the school newspaper and marketing. She sacrifices one vacation day per month for this office - more than she will take on vacation for the entire year. In long meetings, she explains to the school principal how the newspaper could be better designed. And in the end, she has to implement what he wants. At least this honorary position is more fun than her job as a class mom two years ago. She had to coordinate and discuss all sorts of things with twenty other mothers almost every day via Line (a chat app similar to WhatsApp popular in Japan and other Asian countries).

In the afternoon, her son goes straight from elementary school to cram school, like all his classmates. Here, in special shifts, they practice reading and, above all, writing the Japanese script, an important admission criterion for good private schools after elementary school. Their daughter is cared for in the state-run daycare center until seven o'clock.

After the long meeting of the school newspaper committee, she rides her Mamachari, a Japanese electric-assisted bicycle with two child seats, first to pick up her son from his tutoring session, balances the twenty-five-kilo child on the back seat, pedals to the daycare center, packs her fifteen-kilo daughter into the front seat, and then arrives back home around 7:30 p.m.. Now she has to make dinner, and then it's time for a good night's sleep.

As is customary for mothers in Japan, Ayumi and her children sleep together in one bed. Since they only have one bedroom, her husband sleeps in the same room. However, he sleeps on his own futon on the floor so that he is not disturbed by the children at night.

Ayumi just has to be careful not to accidentally kick him when she gets up again at 4:30 in the morning to make bento boxes.

Working mothers everywhere in the world have to be highly organized and hard-working, no question about it. But in Japan, this role is definitely a bit more thankless than in many other regions of the world.

Now why did I speak of "matriarchy" at the beginning of this chapter? Very many Japanese women take on the role described above and fight their way through all the demands made on them and their good behavior in society. However, the supposed oppressor, the husband, then fades far into the background. A Japanese proverb says "A good husband is healthy and absent". This also means: He should please not disturb the home. Disappearing in the morning, earning money, not coming home too early and playing sports on the weekend is indeed the lifestyle of millions of Japanese men, while their wives organize themselves and the children past and around the men.

Interestingly, men's salaries and the household finances are very often managed by their wives. Completely. The men receive a monthly allowance from their wives with which they have to cover the many nomikais and their other leisure activities.

Does that sound incredible? Here are two concrete examples of the interaction of the sexes in 21st century Japan:

During the COVID-19 pandemic, for the first time in living memory, many office workers in Japan, the salarymen already mentioned several times, had to work from home. The wives suddenly had a man sitting in the living room, which was actually theirs and, if necessary, that of the children from early in the morning until late at night. And they did not want to accept this unfamiliar occupant in their small apartment. That's why many men I know personally had to set up their home office in the closet. They disappeared there at nine in the morning, came out briefly for lunch if necessary, and sat in the closet again until the evening. Now Japanese closets are quite large and almost a meter deep, because you store futons in them. But still, they are cramped and windowless cubes constructed not as home offices, but as mattress storage. But before artificial backgrounds became prevalent in video conferencing, I clearly had a lot of digital meetings with men in closets.

The other example shows very nicely how problems are elegantly circumnavigated in Japan instead of being discussed or remedied at the root. And that is with: Salary accounts. The HR director of an international corporation once explained to me at a dinner in Nagoya that his company was active in over one hundred countries. In each of these countries, the salary is transferred to exactly one salary account.

Except in Japan. Here, employees can have their salary paid out spread over up to seven different accounts. The reason for this is that Japanese employees can traditionally hide part of their monthly salary from their strictly bookkeeping spouses in this way. Thus, if the allowance allocated by the matriarchy is too tight, parts of salary increases and bonuses can be elegantly diverted in this way, with the full support of the company, to a use outside the sphere of influence of the partner.

When the Seriousness of Life Begins at Three - Childhood in Japan

Japanese young people spend a very large part of their time in schools. About two hundred and forty days a year are spent in class, compared with about one hundred and ninety days in Europe and the USA. As a result, these institutions are largely responsible for integrating young people into Japanese society with all its complexity, collectivism, and strict hierarchies.

I have already mentioned a first principle of school education, uniformity. Almost all schools prescribe the clothing of their students, in some cases even their hairstyles and hair color. In addition, there are many other rules ranging from the type of umbrella to be used on the way to school to bans on chewing gum between the front door and the school door or the commandment never to sit down on buses and trains. The latter as a sign of deference to adults, even when there are enough seats for everyone. Students are easily assigned to individual schools by their uniforms, and no one is to tarnish the school's reputation by potentially disorderly behavior.

As a rule, a normal school day does not end with the end of the lesson. First, all students clean their classrooms, and on some days they also clean the schoolyard or the school's gardens and hedges. Then the weekly or daily club activities begin. For example, you can belong to a sports club, the school newspaper, the computer club, and so on. Some of these club activities, especially sports, take place every day, throughout the school year and sometimes during the vacations.

At the same time, a very clear seniority principle applies in all school clubs. While the students in their classes are all the same age and all follow the teacher, there is a more complex social structure in the clubs. Students of different ages meet here, and throughout, the younger ones have to treat the older ones with a great deal of respect. According to reports, children in their first year at their school's tennis club or baseball club do nothing but hand water bottles to the older grades and pick up the balls they play with. Then, when they themselves eventually get older, they expect this behavior accordingly from the then youngest club members. This strict system follows the idea of "seishin kyoiku", the education of the mind through discipline and perseverance.

In my eyes, the school clubs are a good key to understanding the Japanese working world. As in the clubs, age and the date of entry into a company are extremely important in many Japanese companies. The two together determine to a good extent social rank within departments and between colleagues. What you learn in your school's sports club at age 10 can thus be applied over and over again until you retire beyond your 60th birthday.

But back to school. When club time also comes to an end in the afternoon, students leave the school grounds. In many cases, though, it's not home. Now it's off to tutoring. Tutoring schools form a very dense parallel school network all their own in Japan. There are tens of thousands of them, in various sizes and with different focuses. More than half of our sons' kindergarten friends already went to tutoring schools. And this carries through to the entrance exams for universities.

Why do children in a highly developed country with two hundred and forty school days a year now have to go to cram schools? There are several reasons for this. First and foremost are the admission requirements for good schools. International schools, private elementary schools, private high schools, even state high schools, and all universities require certain scores on nationally standardized admissions tests. The higher the school's rank in various ratings, the more points are required there for a successful application. Kids have to get into this race very early because if they don't pass the entrance exam for the top elementary school, it becomes harder to get into a top high school. And thus, almost impossible to get accepted to a top university.

Another reason for the many cram schools is that state schools are very poor at teaching foreign languages. Internationally oriented parents are aware of this, and therefore they have their children learn additional English in the afternoon.

Or the children are already in an English-speaking kindergarten so that they can grow up bilingual. Then, in turn, their parents send them to an intensive Japanese course in the afternoons so that their native language doesn't miss out alongside English. It's incredible, but really one back and forth between different educational institutions. Every day.

The financial outlay for private kindergartens, private schools and private tutoring schools is enormous. A really well-off Japanese friend calculated that he was paying about thirty percent of his net monthly salary for his two children's international private school. A co-worker of mine paid as much as ninety percent of her salary for her son's very prestigious private school, and the family covered all other expenses from the husband's salary.

Where does this remarkable willingness to pay for education come from? In addition to the race for the best university places, which begins in kindergarten, it is certainly the enormously high value placed on any kind of education in Japan. Teachers of all kinds, from private tutors to university professors, are highly respected in their roles and are always addressed with a title of honor. While one normally puts a -san after each name, comparable to our title "Mr. X" and "Ms. Y," teachers are given the honorary title -sensei. Pronounced sen-say. So not Spelten-san, but Spelten-sensei. In the Western world this was or is perhaps still usual with professor titles, but in Japan every language teacher, every piano teacher and every yoga trainer is a "sensei" in his or her function, and this honorary title is also used consistently.

I read another reason in a Stanford University study on Japanese education. There it was described that in the Japanese culture it is basically assumed that all students have the same talent at the time of birth, without intellectual differences. Therefore, the general understanding is that it is only the diligence of the individual that determines his or her academic career. And those who do not achieve good grades are simply too lazy. No wonder, then, that parents would rather invest many thousands of euros a year in tutoring than let their child fall behind the group.

In addition to all the above-mentioned school education and sports, there is also cultural and musical education. Here, too, the importance in Japanese society seems to be much higher than in the West, perhaps comparable to bourgeois European families in the past.

In my immediate working environment, all employees without exception had piano lessons as children. And they did so continuously from elementary school through high school graduation. In addition, all but one of the women in this group had additional ballet lessons from elementary school through at least the beginning of high school.

And this tradition continues. Almost all of our sons' kindergarten friends were already taking piano lessons at the age of 3. And without exception, all the girls in the kindergarten group went to ballet. Several of our Japanese friends, who valued culture and could somehow afford it, had a grand piano in their living room. Mind you, in a Japanese living room in Tokyo. The instrument often took up a third of the room or even more.

Even on vacation, many Japanese parents are eager to learn music. When we once spent a week in a hotel on Hokkaido, I saw a grand piano in a lounge area. I thought that was a nice thing and imagined that some talented employee would play some background music for an hour every evening. Far from it. The grand piano was exclusively for guests. Our boys jumped on it enthusiastically the first day, using various body parts to press lively combinations of white and black keys, which of course created a complete cacophony. As parents, we found this very creative, blithely taking photos of our little Mozarts and having a good time. Around us, however, there was an awkward silence.

After we had taken a seat at a table with the boys and two cups of cocoa, a girl of elementary school age sat down at the grand piano and effortlessly played large parts of a piano sonata by Beethoven. I almost fell off my chair. It continued at this level all evening and throughout the vacation. We held our boys reverently away from the grand piano, while there again and again young Japanese between six and sixteen gave complete pieces to the best.

Sometimes with strict parents and score, sometimes alone and from memory. But it should also be said that young pianists almost never seemed relaxed. It always seemed as if they were constantly thinking about the admonitions of their music teachers at home: music is culture, music must be perfect, and mistakes are only made by those who are too undisciplined to play flawlessly.

As fascinating as all my insights into the Japanese education system have been, I unfortunately can't find much positive in it. On the contrary, it puts enormous pressure on children and also their parents. I also think it's one of the main reasons why many Japanese today have such a hard time with cross-hierarchical teams, innovation processes and also the English language. The system takes no account of individual needs and imposes a very tight educational corset on all children.

What I admired in Japan, however, was the enormous willingness of parents to put their children's education above almost everything else. It was not uncommon for them to forego larger apartments, a car or a vacation so that the child could go to a better school, learn more international subjects or get a broader orientation.

Most importantly, by looking at the school system in Japan and the pressures on children there, one gains the impression that the much-maligned, but much more student-centered and often free public K-12 education systems in the West do have great value.

The hard rules in Japanese sports clubs

After we had settled in Tokyo, we thought about enrolling the family in a sports club. Accordingly, I went out and talked to numerous parents at our sons' daycare, colleagues and neighbors to find suitable clubs. The answer I got, succinctly summarized, "Willem-san, don't bother". It turns out that sports clubs are very serious business in Japan both for children, as well as for their parents. In a sports club you don't have to "work your way up" like you do in a school sports team, but here, too, there are often strict rules for everyone involved, and there are lots of honorary positions and numerous tasks for the parents of children who play sports.

Unlike in schools and daycare centers, there are even tasks for fathers in sports clubs., so a family can share the load a little better here – usually only one parent has to take on a function. Nevertheless, there are quite clear gender roles when supporting the baseball team or the soccer team. Fathers, for example, take on the duty of maintaining the field's grass on a weekly basis. Mothers, on the other hand, are given the task of washing the jerseys of all the children, or at least all the coaches, after each practice and bringing them back freshly cleaned the next time.

In addition to cleaning around 30 jerseys and many other tasks, some traditional clubs also have parents cook for the coaching staff every weekend. The mother on duty better does her best, because according to reports, there can be problems if the coaches don't like the food they bring (your child may not see any playing time for several weeks, at worst).

Not every club demands as much support as washing or cooking. Roughly speaking, there are more conservative associations that require a lot of commitment from families, as well as more progressive or service-oriented associations where this is not the case. However, it takes time and effort to understand the peculiarities and demands of each club. If you don't speak Japanese well and don't know anyone in such an association personally, it is very difficult to understand the various rights and obligations.

For this reason, many clubs are not interested in accepting foreigners. Of course, it helps if you or your children are already very good at a sport, like soccer or baseball. But even then, the many social relationships and rules in club life are so important that you quickly fail without good language skills. Legendary in Japan in this context are various foreign athletes who have been hired in recent decades by Japanese professional teams for their brilliant athletic skills. Then, after a few months in Japan, they often flee back to their home country, left miserable because they simply didn't understand the rules, routines and unwritten laws in the complex social ecosystem of their sport.

Of course, there is a wide spectrum of clubs, as previously mentioned. In more modern clubs with fewer parental tasks, everyone washes their own clothes, the coaches' food comes from either a caterer or from the coach himself. But even in the supposedly more modern clubs, the clock sometimes ticks much differently than sports clubs in the West. A friend of mine told me the following story from his son's generally very modern, parent-friendly baseball club: A new coach had been hired, very experienced and about seventy years old. In his inaugural speech, the new coach told the assembled parents, "I understand that you are taking a modern approach to your club, and I approve. Therefore, if the kids make an effort with me, you will never see me beat them. I only do that for laziness or really stupid mistakes."

No one said anything in response. My friend said he was so perplexed that he wasn't sure he had understood correctly. But after several other parents assured him that he had translated everything correctly, he took the coach aside and told him that he would report any blow against his son immediately. Which, by all accounts, the coach forbore to do. My friend's son was not beaten after that, maybe because he managed to avoid any stupid mistakes...?

In addition to baseball, soccer and the popular American football, in Japan are also considered very strict and often exhausting for the entire family involved. Accordingly, these sports are also known for a particularly strong esprit de corps and cohesion among all members. A bit like brotherhoods or sisterhoods, which you work your way into and that accompany you throughout your life.

For those who want to do typical sports in Japan with a little less effort, Kyudo, or archery, is a good option for parents and children alike. Judo and Karate are also of course quite accessible in many dojos in Japan. In addition to hard training and great discipline, these martial arts do not entail too many social obligations.

A special role is played by the Boy Scouts, which I also took a look at. In the urban jungle of Tokyo, I thought, scouts would be a great leisure activity for our sons. However, several Japanese friends clearly shook their heads at the idea. Scouts are quite common in Japan, but they have a very conservative image and are not considered a typical leisure activity for foreign children.

Whereas in Germany scouting was where retired, formerly peace-loving environmentalists would lead a crowd of rather casually uniformed scouts in baking breadsticks, Japanese scouts in tight-fitting uniforms meet on Sundays in the nearest public park, gather around a Japanese flag they bring with them and sing the national anthem. This can certainly bring a lot of joy, but did not fit so well for us.

According to my research, golfing as a club sport is actually the easiest to manage. Here, high fees buy you freedom from most obligations, the coach doesn't expect a hot meal and you're not allowed to mow the lawn, even if you really want to. Unfortunately, we have no interest in golf at all.

Therefore, in the end, our children did not join any sports club, my wife and I kept fit by running and cycling, and as a family we kept a lot of freedom for our weekends. Still, I don't want to discourage anyone from taking on the adventure of a Japanese sports club! On the contrary, for sure you learn many exciting things there in many ways. For me and for us, it just didn't make sense during our time in Tokyo.

The complex world of Japanese friendships

Japan’s omnipresent politeness makes it easy to get into a friendly conversation with Japanese people. However, this usually remains not only friendly, but also at arm’s length. Getting a step ahead here and building a personal bond takes a lot of time and lots of gifts.

Through our children's daycare, we were fortunate to come into daily contact with many Tokyo families very quickly. Since it was an international daycare center, most of the parents also spoke English well, so it was easy to make small talk while dropping off or picking up our kids. After finding two pairs of parents who were particularly congenial, we arranged a playdate at a nearby park and met there on a sunny Saturday afternoon with our total of six children. At this first meeting, the Japanese moms had prepared such an elaborate picnic that we felt completely out of place with our sandwiches and a package of cookies. Each of our new acquaintances had brought five or more homemade dishes to share: hot soup, chicken skewers, fresh onigiri, steamed vegetables, baked sweet potatoes, and more. There were also drinks of various kinds, as well as plates and cutlery for everyone.

Our first afternoon of playing together was so nice that we subsequently met more and more often and made many trips together around Tokyo. As we got to know each other better, our new friends’ lunch spreads became progressively easier, until at one point we were all sitting together on the beach, the children playing in the sea, and each family happily eating ready-made konbini food they had just bought.

As long as we didn't know each other well, they wanted to be polite and bring especially good food, being too embarrassed to present ready-bought products. Politeness, respect and saving face in order to be perfect mothers were so important at first that they spent several hours in the kitchen preparing lunch before our first outings.

Another important dimension of getting to know each other is gifts. At the first meeting, I mentioned how ingenious I thought our friends' ready-made coffee filters were. I had never seen them before, a Japanese specialty: small, individually wrapped coffee filters including coffee powder and a cardboard holder that are packaged to be waterproof. You can simply unfold them on the go, place them on a cup, and brew exactly one cup of fresh steaming coffee with hot water from the thermos. The next Monday, I was handed a sample pack of ten of these little filters by our new friends at daycare. My wife, in turn, had casually mentioned that we miss some cheeses in Japan. She was given a large bag of sinfully expensive cheese from a small dairy store in Naka Meguro, which we should definitely try.

Those who like and want to get closer in Japan usually do so through small gifts, particularly food. These gifts are about showing that you are attentive, you listen to what the others like and then conjure that up at the next meeting, beautifully packaged, from your backpack.

In return, of course, we gave our Japanese friends various things. If someone praised our bread several times at a picnic, we gave them a whole loaf of it at the next meeting, nicely packaged as a souvenir. If our boys' small toy cars were praised for their good quality, we imported a handful of German "Siku" models for the Japanese children.

Quite fundamentally, in Japan you simply have to be aware that gifts are something reciprocal and ongoing. They nurture relationships and friendships and should not be forgotten - because Japanese friends are guaranteed not to forget them.

When you receive a gift, you also give something back. When an opportunity for a small gift arises, you also take that chance. Always. And if one should be invited to an official occasion, such as a wedding, then one must definitely inquire what kind of gift and what value is appropriate here. "Appropriate" is synonymous with "expected" on such official occasions, and it would be very rude not to meet those expectations just as all the other guests do.

Sometimes the very pronounced gift culture produces strange blossoms. For example, we gave various little things on the occasion of an acquaintance giving birth. At our next meeting with the young parents, all of our gifts were stowed away in the stroller as if by pure chance or were in use directly on the child, so that we could easily see that they were really all being used. From the rubber giraffe to the spit-up cloth, everything was clearly visible in use. There was no talk about it - nevertheless, it could not be a coincidence. Especially not because even our gift bag from the Takashimaya department store was dangling from the handlebars of the stroller, wrinkle-free and clearly visible. In addition, we received a bottle of sake back from our friends that day, also in a Takashimaya bag as a thank you for the gifts we gave them. One can continue this cycle of gifts almost endlessly.

As our relationships with various Japanese friends solidified, our conversations became deeper and more personal. This is, of course, almost always the case when you make friends anywhere in the world. But in Japan, the difference between before and after, the contrast with the polite aloofness at the beginning of our relationships, was very great. After many activities together, many gifts, and much time spent together, it was possible, for example, to talk critically about some of the goings-on at the daycare center. This was unthinkable over a period of more than a year ago. A daycare center is an educational institution, and you don't criticize education. At least not until you trust your counterpart very much.

As a parent representative in Germany, I had discussed criticism of various decisions of the kindergarten management (kindergarten is what we call daycare for young children in Germany) with other parents within a few minutes, virtually between door and door. In Japan, this took more than twelve months.

In the same way, we talked with our friends about children, careers, family developments and challenges, social expectations, politics and some gossip. All the topics that you also like to discuss at home with friends, but also acquaintances or other parents in the environment of a daycare center. At some point, everything was more or less the same as with German friends. But only after a very long period of cautious rapprochement, of slowly getting to know each other, of building trust and of unspoken proof of honest interest in each other through a multitude of small gifts and attentions.

Work and work culture in Japan

The office - the center of many Japanese lives

The life of a Japanese professional usually begins on April 1. Throughout the country, this is the day when graduates of trade schools and universities are welcomed to festive entrance ceremonies by CEOs, chairmen and managing directors. This important day is preceded by lengthy application and selection processes, often a full year in advance.

The entire cohort with which you start in a new company will accompany you throughout the rest of your professional life in that company. You are part of a certain cohort that starts its professional life together and now goes through different trainings and areas of the new company as a group. In the best-case scenario, you will also find your spouse in this cohort, but in any case you will find some confidants and friends.

Once you have made it into a large and prestigious company, you will find yourself doing a wide variety of jobs there over the following years and decades. HR tends to promote generalists rather than specialists and will happily transfer employees to different departments, as well as subsidiaries and other countries. And even though this form of employment is no longer as common as it was a few decades ago, it is still considered desirable to stay with the same employer for life. This is reinforced by the fact that the professional environment, especially one's immediate colleagues and even the starting cohort, are seen as an extended family. You grow into this close network of relationships, find your position and develop within the system. A so-called mid-career move is much more common now than in the past and can pay off handsomely financially, but it puts enormous social pressure on the individual that is hard to imagine in the West. Work is still an eminently important part of social life in Japan, and changing companies sometimes feels like cheating on previous colleagues for those affected.

The regular working day in Japan for office workers officially lasts from nine in the morning until five or six in the evening.

However, especially in traditional Japanese companies, employees often sit at their desks for much longer, either because the boss hasn't left yet, or because their colleagues haven't left yet. Basically, most workers are tied to their desks till late because someone is still there whom they don't want to disappoint.

In addition, overtime is often paid, sometimes even with bonuses. Therefore, there is also a monetary incentive to work a little longer. The working hours themselves don't necessarily have to be particularly productive - in Japan, I sometimes had the impression that at some of the desks in our open-plan office, people were deliberately idling away the morning on the Internet in order to then get on with their day's work in the evening during the extra paid overtime. In addition, some male colleagues faced the challenge that their wives did not want to see them at home before eight o'clock in the evening. Accordingly, they also tried not to finish their work too early.

Of course, there are also vacation days in Japan. The law provides for a minimum of ten paid vacation days per year for a full-time job, and each year the number grows by one or two more days, until after seven years you have accumulated around twenty vacation days. Add sixteen public holidays per year, and that still adds up to thirty-six days off. That's not bad in and of itself. Compare this to the U.S., with many employees only having fifteen days of paid vacation and eleven holidays after ten years on the job. In Japan, however, there are two challenges. First, there is no sick pay. That's why many employees use up part of their vacation time when they get sick.

On the other hand, people simply don't like to take vacation. The background here is that individual vacation leads to extra work and stress among colleagues. And you don't want that, because harmony is important, and the whole group shouldn't suffer because of your own supposedly selfish wish for a vacation. That's why they pull themselves together with their team and prefer not to take the vacation.

A close friend of ours once told me that after about five years on the job, she had taken two weeks of saved-up vacation at a time to visit her partner's family in Europe. She said she felt bad and unfair for the whole fortnight because she had left her colleagues behind with all the work. And this friend was not yet thirty years old, had studied in the U.S., was engaged to a European, and was definitely not a conservative representative of "Old Japan." But politeness, consideration for the group and putting individual needs aside are simply very deeply anchored in many Japanese.

With recurring reports of deaths from overwork, an occurrence known as "karoshi," in Japan, the government has taken various measures in recent years to combat overzealousness at work. For one thing, power harassment is now heavily addressed, and managers must be careful not to put unfair pressure on their teams. Second, all employers must now ensure that every employee takes at least five full days of vacation per year.

Five days doesn't sound like much, especially if you include sick days. Nevertheless, there are often problems complying with this strict and punitive legal requirement. Since employees sometimes have to be literally forced to take vacation, some offices are now simply closed the week after Christmas so that everyone working there automatically takes five days of vacation before the deadline on December 31 of each year. This arrangement is again quite popular with the employees, since in this case all colleagues do not work, so no one else can suffer if you yourself are not present.

The course of a working day in Japan naturally varies greatly depending on the job. But at the large companies that are so popular, the work environment surprisingly often looks similar. In huge open-plan offices, you take a seat at a long row of desks. There are often ten desks in two rows next to each other, resulting in twenty workstations close together. Then comes two meters of space to move office chairs back and forth. Followed by the next battery of twenty seats. These rows of desks extend so deep into the building that in some high-rise office buildings you can barely see daylight at the last few desks. You can see the window front twenty meters away, of course, but without fluorescent light you sit in twilight all day.

Comparing the set-up of open-plan offices in different countries, I would estimate that Japan certainly has twice as many people working in the same office space as American offices with their "cubicles", and at least three times as many people working in all the German open-plan offices I have seen so far.

Yet Japanese offices are not only very crowded, but also very uninspired and sometimes downright repulsive. There is no sign of the great Japanese interior design tradition or traditional harmony here. A Japanese office is usually a loveless and functional space where a great many people spend most of their waking lives. And no matter how prestigious the lobbies or meeting floors of many Japanese companies are, most of the work is usually done on completely unadorned floor space.

Their low attractiveness stems not only from the cramped conditions, but also from the furnishings. In particular, office chairs from before the turn of the millennium, still very often in use, have a negative influence here. For some reason, they are almost always upholstered in a baby-blue or lime-green fabric, which is found not only in older facilities, but also in pretty modern offices. On the chair backs, this fabric is always significantly darker, because it has been touched here for twenty years and more... These colors are particularly awful when there are additional sound-absorbing walls between some desks in open-plan offices. Because then they are also upholstered in the same fabric as the seat cushions and welcome you with many square meters of color mood.

If you like lime green a lot, you might wonder why I used the word "repulsive." It doesn't stem at all from the questionable choice of color in many offices, but from their degree of wear and tear. Similar to houses, which in Japan are torn down after about thirty years, as described above, the motto seems to apply to the entire interior decoration of offices and official rooms, namely that they should not be renovated.

Nicotine-yellow fax machines, carpeting with stains and holes under the wheelchairs, visibly worn office chair backs and worn-through, holey office chair cushions are no exception, but a fixed part of everyday business life in many offices in Japan. At the municipal office in our district, where about fifteen civil servants worked, the neon lamps hung from the ceiling as crookedly as if they had not been screwed back on after the last earthquake. At the headquarters of a major Japanese insurance company, the office walls had visibly not been painted in decades and were full of welts and scratches. And in the Japanese Ministry of Transport, I sat in offices that looked as if they had not been cleaned even once in many years, neither by the officials working here nor by any cleaning staff.

Of course, there are also modern and renovated offices. These are then furnished with fancy furniture, and in new buildings every space has daylight and you can work well there. But even there, the areas are usually very densely packed and there is little space and peace for individual employees. With the exception of Google's head office in Shibuya, I didn't see any offices that really made me want to work in Japan.

Efficiency, inefficiency and digitalization

The high regard that Japan is sometimes held in as an efficient country of cutting technology is often simply wrong. In fact, it is a country that masterfully combines tradition and modernity by means of sophisticated and sprawling processes. Which is impressive, but also leads to absurd situations time and again.

Japan has certainly produced fascinating technological solutions. Japanese hybrid vehicles are economical and inexpensive, the metro and express train network is unbelievably good and efficient, and cell phones can be used to make calls in every tunnel, forest and express train, while in New York even on the Long Island Railroad passengers experience signal loss a few times per hour of travel. But behind these outstanding examples of great technology comes a long time - nothing.

If you have ever looked at websites of Japanese hotels or restaurants to prepare for your vacation, you will get an impression of this reality. Most of these websites look like they were first designed around the time of the dotcom bubble and then never touched again. Unfortunately, this pattern continues in everyday life when online in Japan. It is particularly painful on the online banking pages of Japanese financial institutions. Apart from the fact that many pages are not available in English and, among other things, require the input of Japanese characters to execute a transfer, they also tend to branch out into unimaginable depths. At the same time, these pages are as attractively designed as the fine print on the back of a used car sales contract.

The most ubiquitous artifact of Japan's backwardness when it comes to digitization, and one that is often smiled at in disbelief by newcomers to the country, is the fax machine. While these devices have been scrapped for years in most parts of the world, they still rattle merrily in nearly every Japanese office. There are various reasons for this, such as a deep trust in and reverence for paper, and the physical filing of documents. And the adherence to the tried and tested processes that the most senior office workers learned when they started their jobs (often at the same company) forty years ago.

The fax drama also has a lot to do with how many documents are attested in Japan. Because in Japan, you often don't sign documents, you stamp them with a personal, unique stamp. called a hanko. Almost every resident of Japan has such a hanko, the imprint of which you have to register with your local municipality. As a rule, hankos are carved by hand so that they are truly unique, just like a signature. In addition to personal hankos, there are also corporate hankos with different levels of importance and attestation rights. At the very top of the stamp importance pyramid is the main seal of a company. With it, large payments and extensive contracts can be released.

With the outbreak of the COVID-19 pandemic, Japanese companies were faced with the huge problem that there was often no digital way whatsoever to release important contracts or payment orders without the company's main seal. This all-important hanko is stored in a secure vault in the company building and is usually pressed several times a week by a high-ranking member of the legal or finance department on all necessary documents while sitting right next to the safe. And afterwards these stamped documents are then sent where they need to go by fax.

As a result, even during Japan's strict lockdowns, a few employees per company were compelled to go into the office to stamp papers, and in other companies, employees sat at the fax machines to receive these stamped documents.

The Japanese government has had a Minister for Digital Transformation who leads the Digital Agency and reports directly to the Prime Minister since the summer of 2021, so the problem has been recognized in principle. However, its employees still have a long way to go, and are currently discussing the introduction of digital signatures in PDF documents.

In addition to sophisticated computers and the latest consumer electronics, many expect to see robots on every corner in Japan. As a normal visitor, however, you only really see them in action in one place: the "Robot Restaurant" in Shinjuku, a musical theater in which the robots do little more than flash colorfully or are controlled by costumed humans on stage.

Apart from Shinjuku's robot show, you'll more than likely stumble across "Pepper" every now and then, the service robot presented at great expense by Softbank in 2014. These white plastic-clad cute little guys look very friendly, wear a tablet computer on their chests and are supposed to be able to recognize the emotions of their counterparts.

Pepper was primarily developed for use at information desks, and so you see one every now and then in train stations, tourist information offices, hotels or even supermarkets. Unfortunately, Pepper never really works. After a short conversation they go mute and start looking right and left sadly - or they just fall asleep and stand around as expensive dust collectors.

Basically, my impression was that the combination of Japan and robots is a completely unjustified legend. There are always exaggerated or even false reports in Western media about the use of some prototype robots in Japan, but these usually have little substance. For example, one newspaper reported that a twenty-meter-tall walking robot had been developed in Japan. This was, in actuality, an amusement park attraction, and the "robot" can do little more than lift its feet and move its hands in a photogenic manner. Similarly, there have been reports of a cuddly robot that supposedly gives emotional attention to handicapped or bedridden people in Japan. The reality is that this robot was only a one-off and was basically an experiment behind the plexiglass of a museum showcase. One could also claim that Elon Musk's Hyperloop is actually running.

Let's move on from robots to efficiency once again. Japanese media sometimes speak of "typically Japanese efficient inefficiency". What is this? The hankos are certainly a good example. Because you don't address the basic problem, the need for a physical seal, you create sophisticated (or overly complicated) solutions, like fax machines, that implement a new, modern, process while doing nothing to eliminate the old, outdated process.

There was a similarly creative solution under the COVID-19 entry rules. After landing in Japan, returnees from abroad had to go through a maze of small stations in an empty terminal and complete a wide variety of administrative tasks. A docket was used to ensure that no traveler got lost. They started at station one and slowly made their way to station seven, where a COVID-19 quick test was carried out.

The astonishing thing was the opaque logic of the procedures, some of which were repeated at different stations. Didn't I just fill out a questionnaire about my place of residence and now I have to do it again? And then again at the next station, a third time, with only slightly different questions than before? Why didn't any of the stations want to see the PCR rapid test that had been collected so expensively before departure? Instead, they asked for my passport, at the next station for my residence permit, and at another station only for the flight tickets.

The background was that each of the stations was run by a different ministry or state institution. Each party had specific interests, its own documentation and had not linked themselves in any way in terms of content or organization with the other state organs present. Therefore, at each individual station, only what the respective authority found useful for its purposes was queried, and at the same time, the same basic questions were asked again at each station. All this was done in a very friendly manner and with a lot of patience. One felt quite welcome as a traveler given the character of the staff, but was left wondering what on earth was happening. There was also no information about who you were talking to or why.

This uncoordinated interaction of the various institutions was clarified months later by an article in *The Japan Times*. The reactions of various letter writers were very similar. People literally grabbed their heads at the complexity and effort involved, but no one was really surprised by this perfectly organized, completely inefficient approach by the authorities.

Celebrating at the end of the day - Nomikais and social outing

In Japan, drinking or getting drunk with colleagues is called nomikai and is certainly one of the country's best-known cultural characteristics. I heard about it many years ago, probably on a TV news program. Then at school and college, one of the few things you learned about Japan was the story about drinking after hours and that you could only tell your boss the truth when you were drunk. I was correspondingly anxious before my own first nomikai. How much of the cliché corresponded to the truth? And what were Western exaggerations of the exotic Orient, increasingly distorted by word of mouth and far removed from reality? To whit: Nothing was distorted, everything was true. Nomikai means pressure refueling, battle drinking and drunkenness for a maximum of two hours. But it's accompanied by good food and, to be honest, it's a lot of fun. For me, a business day usually started with me at the office alone around eight in the morning. This was less due to my enormous diligence than to the fact that I only needed fifteen minutes to get from home to work. Around nine o'clock, I was joined by my colleagues who had further commutes. Each of them entered the room, called out "Ohayou Gozaimass" (good morning) once, and sat down. Silence reigned for the next four hours, with the occasional phone call. During the lunch break, we all had a lively chat in the canteen and caught up on the small talk that we would have had in a Western office early in the morning.

In the afternoon, the mood was a little more relaxed, and there was also a bit of talking across table boundaries. But it was still very quiet in our open-plan office, very concentrated and all in all very impersonal. That is, until it was finally seven o'clock. Time to go for a drink!

For my first nomikai, we met within walking distance of our office at a small Japanese pizzeria. My team had already ordered us tabehodai for us, i.e. a flat rate with food and drinks. Since I was still on the phone, I was the last to arrive at the restaurant.

Everyone was already seated at two large tables, eating pizza and drinking themselves silly. Usually they do this with highballs, the true Japanese national drink. Highballs in Japan consist of some whisky, maybe two fingers high, and soda water. It has the reputation of having far fewer calories than beer and wine, despite its intense effect, and is therefore very popular. And it tastes great once you get used to the taste of diluted Suntory whisky.

So my colleagues drank highballs, along with a draft beer here and there ("Nama!" More on that in the language chapter) or sometimes a glass of red wine. To put it bluntly: all of this was consumed simultaneously, up to three glasses in front of each person at a time. That's what I meant by effect drinking. The almost two hours of the tabehodai package are used quite consistently to get full and drunk. Each and every person steers the goal individually according to their own capacities and the mood of the day. I sat down next to my colleague Noriko with her two big glasses of red wine and a highball next to the pizza and joined with a beer, which was to be my rather epic first night out with the team.

I'll skip a lot of details now with consideration for people who are still alive and whom I hold in high esteem. In any case, we managed to make good use of our flat rate. When the waitress announced "last order," everyone ordered several more drinks for the last half hour - and so we left the pizzeria at nine o'clock in high spirits. We had already loudly reviewed the work experiences of the first weeks since my arrival in Japan, laughed at some cultural missteps of mine, and had been blithely banging on about other departments and our company itself. All of this was actually unthinkable in the office and now bubbled out of everyone after the first drink. The basic hierarchy of the department remained the same, by age and rank. This was evident in who topped up whose drink, or who caught a completely off-topic discussion after all. But all in all, my Japanese team was as fun and easy-going as I had hoped for in the office, but had never come close to experiencing.

After the pizzeria, it was off to karaoke. Many karaoke bars have a reputation for purposefully fleecing their customers in their increasingly relaxed moods by increasing room rental rates on a logarithmic scale: A thousand yen for the first thirty minutes, two thousand for the next half hour, and then five thousand yen per half hour following. And of course drinks are extra. Fortunately, we were still fit enough not to fall into such a trap. And went to the Japanese market leader: Big Echo. Funny name for a karaoke operator, in whose booths one wants to avoid one thing above all - that two switched on microphones produce an echo ... But I overlook such details now and come back to our night out.

At Big Echo we again ordered a flat rate course, another two hours nomihodai (nomihodai is a drink flat rate, tabehodai includes food). And then we sang. One thing should be noted: Karaoke singing in Japan is a lot of fun, but it is not for fun. Karaoke is a competition, and it is taken very seriously, even when drunk. While an Australian colleague and I were still boisterously belting out old Rolling Stones hits at the beginning, our Japanese colleagues delivered one perfectly sung song after another. Japanese folk songs, Japanese pop hits, a lot of Blackpink and a lot of Britney Spears, all to the exact note and in tune, exactly in time and really nice to listen to.

In my panic of completely embarrassing myself with my bad singing, I desperately searched the online menu of the karaoke machine for some song that I should be able to play back at least passably. Not sung too high, lyrics and melody well known. I finally landed on "Rock Me Amadeus" by Falco. The fact that nobody in the room knew this German (actually, Austrian) world hit from 1985 did not detract from my artistic performance, and I sang or rapped a performance worthy of the Grammys on the plastic parquet. The result of my well-received performance was that from then on, I had to perform this song every time I went to karaoke, and my Japanese colleagues always sang along clapping along with the "Amadeus Amadeus" chorus. Whether this was out of enthusiasm or pity, I will probably never know.

Because karaoke requires skill, many people in Japan like to rent karaoke booths to rehearse on their own. During the daytime prices are quite attractive, and so you can continuously increase your repertoire of songs. If you are traveling in Japan, you should try karaoke as well as the already described pachinko. Even alone or in pairs, just to have experienced it. The procedure is very simple. At the reception desk, make clear how many people are in your group, how long you want to stay first, order a nomihodai if needed, and you get a room number. In the room you have just rented, there is usually a tablet computer that can also be switched to English. It contains the music menu for the large screen on the wall. And the drink menu to make the first attempts at singing more bearable. At the end of the karaoke adventure, you simply go back to the reception, pay your debts and go on your way humming "Amadeus Amadeus”.

The Seniority Principle, Courtesy in Japan and the Happiness of Being Respected

For some years now, there has been an "ikigai" trend in the Western world. "Ikigai" is a Japanese word that means something like "sense of life". Various books with esoteric covers talk about this “sense of life” of the Japanese. And in a particularly popular work, based on interviews with very old people from the Okinawan Islands, the whole thing has become processed (in typical Western fashion) into a kind of guide to becoming a hundred years old.

The vast majority of these books seem to me to interpret quite freely what Japanese themselves consider "ikigai." I have only read a few of them, but often the authors underestimate how important the relationship of the individual to the group is in this context in Japan. Being part of a group or taking responsibility for a group entails many duties, but it also brings belonging, community and the recognition of making a valuable contribution to something bigger. This is what makes people in Japan satisfied who might feel lonely or otherwise not needed in other cultures.

On this point, seniority assumes an important significance. In various chapters, I have already mentioned that, for example, the date of entry into a company over decades can influence tone’s social position in that company, coupled with increasing age and thus seniority level. Similarly, the length of membership in an association combined with one's age also plays an important role. Not to mention the age-dependent relationships in a family, in which, for example, the second-born son is referred to as the younger brother for the rest of his life with the fixed term "jinan," while his older brother will forever be the first-born "chounan."

In companies and associations, people who have been there for a long time are called "senpai" or "senior" and are also addressed with this honorary title. Newcomers, on the other hand, are "kohai" or "junior". In the company, "senpai" are expected to take care of the "kohai" like good mentors. At the same time, it is clear that the "kohai" are subordinate to the senpai and listen to their advice.

It becomes difficult when a colleague who has just joined the company as a so-called "mid-career-hire" is older than his colleagues who work directly with him but have been with the company for longer and are therefore "senpai". For now, he is both "kohai" in terms of length of service, but is still more senior than his new colleagues because of his advanced age. In this case, at least in my company, the more experienced colleagues in the company nevertheless took on the role of mentors. However, they were much more polite and respectful than they usually were toward younger "kohai" newcomers.

This balancing act is difficult for non-Japanese to comprehend and quite difficult to master correctly. And no matter how many times I have looked at such processes around me in the office, I have never quite understood when, how or why one behaves completely correctly in this regard. There are just far too many fine gradations of politeness in daily interactions. It starts early in the morning with the question of who presses the buttons on the elevator (usually the employee who appears youngest by age), to the question of who pours for whom at the evening nomikai (usually everyone without hierarchy, but with larger hierarchy differences then again the lower level employees to their bosses). I should add: if it is not readily apparent who is lowest in age and hierarchy, it will always be a woman who presses the button or pours the drinks. Being female works like an inverted joker when it comes to hierarchy in Japan…

To make matters worse, with all these complex rules of politeness, the use of a very special form of Japanese language comes into play: the so-called "keigo".

Keigo refers to a set of speech forms used to express respect and politeness. "Sonkeigo" is used to express respect for people who are in socially higher positions than the speaker. For example, to express respect for superiors, older people, or customers. "Kenjougo" is used to express respect for people who are in socially lower positions than the speaker. For example, to express respect for subordinates or younger people. The use of keigo is an important aspect of Japanese culture and helps to express respect and politeness in social relationships. Conversely, this also means that you have to be very aware of social relationships in order to choose the right level of linguistic politeness. And then you have to speak and understand Japanese excellently to be able to express that level of language.

In a somewhat simplified way, you can imagine Keigo as saying to a new colleague of a more advanced age not "Please do this and that", but rather "I know you are very busy and I am sorry that I have to disturb you in your stressful everyday life. It would be of a tremendous assistance to me if you could maybe do this or that on occasion. Thank you and please excuse the intrusion."

But what on earth does all this have to do with "ikigai"? Quite simply, the high regard for age, life's work and experience means that old people in Japan are generally highly respected, even if their immediate work performance can no longer keep up with that of younger, more dynamic colleagues. This respect is palpable for senior citizens and is clearly reflected in the behavior and language of younger people toward them.

At the same time, it is important to many Japanese, even in old age, to continue to actively contribute to the well-being of the community and to continue to have a task to perform.

The interaction between the respect of the younger generation, and the hard work and enthusiasm of the older generation results in a win-win situation in which even very old people in Japan are still given tasks that serve the community. And they themselves have the good feeling that they can continue to make a contribution to the greater whole.

We must not paint this principle too rosy, though. Of course, there are also economic constraints in this system, and some octogenarians have to supplement their meager pensions by working paying, but likely part time, jobs every day. But very often, the many working old-age people in Japan are not an expression of a bad social system. Rather, work forms the core of their "ikigai." Instead of boredom and increasing loneliness, they prefer to contribute actively. Be it in return for payment as a senior advisor on the office floors of a company, as a security guard at a road construction site or as an attendant on a school bus. Often also without or with rather symbolic payment as a volunteer in a museum, as a crossing guard at a crosswalk or as part of an amateur gardening collective in a public park.

If you walk through Japan with your eyes open, you will see legions of obviously elderly people everywhere, diligently going about their business. And everyone respects them. Even if waving a flag in front of a highly visible construction site in a small residential street may not make much more sense than keeping the old gentleman well occupied with his little flag.

Japanese people with whom I have talked about "ikigai" books were very surprised that they exist. In Japan itself, "ikigai" is not something that would be widely discussed or even exaggerated as a philosophy that brings happiness. Or as my friend Kazuko put it, "My ikigai is to drink a beer on the sofa in the evening."

How to behave in Japan - best possible

When in doubt - just take off your shoes!

The most important rule of etiquette in Japan? When in doubt, take off your shoes and politely glide into the slippers you're provided. In particular when entering private homes, temples, baths (not toilets, just those rooms used exclusively for bathing) and hotel rooms. Sometimes when entering the seating area of restaurants and the changing areas of stores. And rarely, but still possible, even when entering offices and official rooms.

The fact that Japanese culture places as high a value on cleanliness as probably nowhere else in the world is the most obvious reason for this custom. But there is also the fact that the everyday life of Japanese people traditionally takes place close to or even on the floor. For example, for centuries people ate sitting directly on the floor at low tables. People slept on a futon, which was rolled out on the floor in the evening, and do many things in the house at the warm, cozy kotatsu we talked about earlier.

Social life in Japan historically always took place 18 inches lower than in the Western world with its chairs and high tables and this gave having an impeccably clean floor an even more important, hygienically critical significance than in the West, for example.

Like so many things, shoe management in Japan has of course been perfected over the centuries. Thus, wherever shoes have to be taken off, there is a clearly visible landing of anywhere from a couple of inches to two full steps high that reminds you to "fix your feet" before going any further. The lower area separated by this step directly behind the entrance door is called the "genkan" and forms the transition from the "outside" to the higher, inner living area.

In old Japanese houses, both the exterior of the house and the entrance area consisted of tamped clay. This was partly where the pets lived, and also where heavy and dirty work was done. Sometimes this area also housed some cooking and fireplaces, called kamados.

The actual living area of these old houses was raised just over a foot above the clay floor for the simple reason that for this four tree trunks were joined at their ends into a rectangle and covered with planks and boards. This naturally created the difference in height between the dirty outside and the clean inside, and there was often no wall or door between these worlds. The step regulated this division. In practical terms, it's pretty difficult for dust and dirt to leap up from the lowered genkan into the living space, so those few inches are actually very effective at leveraging gravity to keep the outside mess outside.

On the elevated wooden platform, individual rooms were separated with boards or thin sliding walls made of slats and a paper covering. In some of these rooms simply the planed surface of the planks and boards from which the raised area was constructed formed the floor. This was common, for example, in the living room, often additionally provided with a fireplace embedded in the floor called "irori".

Other rooms were given a more elaborate floor, here mats of woven rice straw, called tatami mats, were additionally laid on the wooden planks. Rooms with these more comfortable mats were used mainly for sleeping, receiving guests and praying in front of the family altar. In simple farmhouses, a single tatami room often fulfilled all these functions at the same time.

Tatami mats are sensitive, especially to moisture, and difficult to clean. Therefore, people traditionally moved in slippers or slippers in all rooms with wooden floors, but walked barefoot or only with socks on tatami. And the same rule applies to this day: shoes off at the entrance, slippers off at tatami.

In addition, there are two special rules for correct footwear. And these apply in the garden and in toilets:

The floor of a toilet is considered very dirty. Traditionally, this may be due to the fact that until a few decades ago, most Japanese toilets were 18 inches closer to the floor as well - they were simply ceramic-encased holes that could flush. Western-style sit-down toilets did not outsell traditional squat-down toilets in Japan till the late 1970s, prior to that being more of an imported luxury home addition.

Even though Japanese toilets today are usually well above the level of the floor, toilet etiquette has persisted. If you go to the toilet in a ryokan, a traditional restaurant, or even some private homes, you will often find one or two pairs of plastic slippers right behind the toilet door. These are not left there by chance, but are the designated toilet footwear. Now you have to take off your own slippers in front of the toilet door without using your hands, slide into the toilet slippers with a daring step, do your business and then change back into your own sandals. It is important to avoid touching the floor outside the wet room with the toilet slippers. The trick is to make a direct foot change from slipper to slipper without any contact with the floor.

Another special sandal is waiting at patio and garden doors. While public interiors usually come with ugly but functional plastic slippers in light brown or green, the gardens often have historic "geta" ready to go. These are traditional sandals that are essentially wooden flip-flops on stilts. Under the sole are two wooden pieces positioned lengthwise so that they raise the user a few inches off the ground, offer some stability and provide a bit of traction. They also make wearing the geta extremely uncomfortable.

With the Geta, you can roam the Japanese garden of your ryokan or, if needed, smoke a cigarette in a quiet corner before heading back inside and slipping back into your plastic sandals just as elegantly and without touching the ground as you did when you went to the bathroom.

All these rules read terribly complicated and somewhat stiff, but once you are in Japan, it all starts to make sense and the adjustment isn’t difficult. You simply have to observe with an alert eye what the people around you are doing and adopt this as best you can. For those who have grown up in Japan, footwear etiquette is such an integral part of their lives that it is basically internalized, and taking off shoes or changing slippers at the right time or situation is a matter of course.

One of our most impressive encounters with the matter-of-factness with which people in Japan simply never enter a house with shoes on was our move-in. Over a period of three days, our six movers in Tokyo transported all of our belongings from a seabound container to our new abode. Among them some were really bulky and heavy furniture like a medieval chest made of more or less petrified oak wood. But no matter how heavy the items were, the gentlemen moving our things quite fluidly and without even stopping stripped off their shoes when entering the house without any interruption, continuing on in their socks into the stairwell and up the stairs. There was no hesitation and no stalling, elegantly merging towing, removing shoes and taking the stairs into a single and very impressive freestyle.

During my time in Japan, I learned to slip off my shoes quickly and easily. With every slip in and out, this also works better as you consistently destroy the heel part of your shoes. At first it resists with stiffness, then it just scratches and after a few weeks it's just a buttery soft shadow of itself.

It's worth taking a look at the shoes on the feet of fellow subway passengers in Japan. For obvious reasons, loafers are extremely popular. There are also lace-up shoes, but they are almost always trampled flat at the heel and correspondingly unsightly.

For these reasons, it is also not particularly useful to start your trip to Japan with 16-hole Doc Martens shoes. Otherwise, you'll tire yourself out and get terribly delayed constantly tying and untying your boots during a visit to a few temples. It's better to pack loafers or reasonably well-trodden sports shoes in your luggage, which you can slip into again and again without much effort.

For obvious reasons, of paramount importance is to wear new socks. Nothing is more embarrassing than trudging through a restaurant with a toe sticking out of your white socks. I emphasize this from personal experience.

Washing, scrubbing and polishing - the art of body care in the onsen

Completely intimidated by the complex instructions in Lonely Planet, Frommer's and Tripadvisor, I sat stark naked on a much too small wooden stool in front of a faucet with a short-hosed shower head at knee height and wondered what the correct washing sequence was. First buttocks, then lower legs soap? Or should we start with the toes? Where did this tiny towel have to go in the shower? And were all the Japanese people in the shower room really looking at me?

Somehow, however, I made it to the onsen. And let the warm water wash away my worries.

Many onsen visits later, I can say two things for sure: first, that you should use any onsen that is available anywhere. And second, that there is far too much fuss about onsen etiquette.

To enjoy an onsen, a traditional Japanese hot spring bath, from the first visit, it is necessary to understand a very simple fact. The onsen consists of several areas, and it is not a sauna. The primary goal of visiting an onsen is to soak, and in order to soak you need to get clean. Very clean. And only when you are clean, really clean as a whistle, do you move from the shower area to the bathing area. Remember: In the West, you bathe to get clean. In Japan, you get clean in order to bathe.

Onsen bathing is different than other bathing for another important reason: the word "onsen" does not refer to the bath itself, but to the natural mineral water that you bathe in at a "real" onsen. In most cases this water is pumped from geothermally heated aquifers at the site of the onsen bath house and mixed with cooler water from public waterways to bring the water to bathable temperatures, but there are cases where natural mineral water is trucked into an urban bath house so that it can be called an "onsen". The specific mineral makeup of the water is also considered very important to determine what specific benefits your bath will bestow on you. Some onsens claim to give you beautiful skin.

Some heal muscle pains. Others reduce blood pressure. And some relieve joint pain. All of these benefits (and more!) are advertised by local government travel offices as well as onsen ryokans themselves to attract customers from Japan and abroad. So, choose your onsen carefully!

But before that, know that there are a few rules. But the whole onsen visit isn't magic, and once you check into a ryokan or hotel with an onsen, you shouldn't let anything stop you from jumping into the washing and bathing fun.

As a rule, one enters the onsen through a door marked with the kanji for "men" or "women", which is often in either blue (for men) or red (for women) color, respectively. Onsen are, in the vast majority of cases, strictly separated by gender, although small children can go with any parent or older family member.

Behind the gender-marked door is a changing area where you disrobe. You should get your towels at the reception, or if not, they will be available here in the changing room. You need a large towel for your body, which you leave with your clothes in a basket, cubby or locker. You also need a small towel, not more than a cloth napkin. This hand towel will accompany you to the shower and wash area, and you can use it as a sort of Garden of Eden-style fig leaf, holding it in front of your private parts as you walk. It won't necessarily cover everything, but having it helps put you at ease while also showing others that you're making an honest effort at modesty.

In the shower room, depending on the size of the onsen, there are anywhere from one to one hundred shower stations just as described previously: Low to the ground, with a faucet, a shower head on a hose, a knob or lever to turn on the water and choose your temperature, and a lever to switch between the faucet and shower head. Sometimes these stations are along a single wall, sometimes there are several built in cross-patterns with shower stations on both sides. These are usually quite close to each other and often not separated by partitions. Those partitions I saw were never higher than 3 feet, serving more as splash guards than privacy barriers. In other words: The shower area of the onsen underscores that this is a PUBLIC bath.

In the shower area, you now select your place of choice. Apart from the position in the room, each place should be identical. At each station you will find, in addition to all the plumbing, a small stool, a large bowl, sometimes a small ball, and always at least three huge bottles of toiletries: Body soap, shampoo and conditioner. Some hotel onsen mean particularly well and also offer more care products, like a file for calluses, combs, sponges or loofahs, or disposable razors.

You simply sit down on the stool provided, fill the large bowl with warm water and pour it over your head and all other parts of your body until you are nice and wet. You could also use the shower head for this, but the risk of splashing others is higher with this method. Besides, it's somehow more fun and feels more “Japanese” to douse yourself with the bowl of water again and again, in particular if it's a traditional wooden bowl made of fragrant cedar instead of a plastic one.

After you are all good and wet, you shampoo your hair and soap yourself with the body soap all over – really, everywhere. Between your toes, behind your ears and of course where the sun doesn’t shine. For this you will have to get up from your stool for a moment.

Then you rinse yourself all over so that no soap suds at all are sticking to your body to complete the basic cleaning. If you have enjoyed this and want to do it especially well, you can just start the whole procedure again from the beginning!

After that, feeling sparkling clean, freed from dirt and soap, comes the grand finale: The soaking – or in some onsen you might call this soft boiling.

To do this, you once again take your hand towel, which hopefully survived the cleaning ritual, and dry your face if necessary. Then you go to one of the onsen pools known as “rotenburo”. Often there are several, and it is useful to pay attention to any temperature indications. In the case of small pools for a single person, you may be able to regulate the temperature for yourself via a faucet at the edge of the pool. If you turn this on, ice-cold water runs out and thereby slowly lowers the temperature of the already collected water. I have also been in onsen that were so hot that I had to first drain half of the available water by pulling the plug, and then fill it up again with ice water. Therefore, my strong recommendation is to first test the water with your finger before you accidentally scald half your body.

When you have found your desired pool, sit down and enjoy! It's traditional to fold your hand towel into a small square and place right atop your head while your entire body from shoulders on down are under the hot water. While this might make you feel (or look) a bit silly, you'll quickly find that the Japanese bathers around you are for the most part doing the same, making you just another part of the crowd. (Congratulations on taking one more step toward Japanese cultural assimilation!)

Alternatively, the towel can simply be placed somewhere on the edge of the pool. However, since it may be a little sweaty or perhaps used to dry the face, it is considered unhygienic if the onsen water touches it. Therefore, one should avoid this from happening.

Though inherently relaxing, a visit to a mid-size or larger onsen ends up being quite busy. There are often several different pools of different sizes, settings, mineral contents and temperatures, not to mention occasional saunas, mist showers and outdoor decks to enjoy in your birthday suit. So, after relaxing in one or more pools, at least, it's back to the changing room with hand towel fig leaf leading the way. Since people from outside Japan often shave their private parts, while Japanese people often don't, you can save yourself a lot of shocked looks from your fellow bathers with a bit of modesty here.

In the changing room there is usually an area with a row of sinks and mirrors, where you can now get gussied up. A hairdryer and a body lotion are usually ready here, often also hair lotion, perhaps and depending on the establishment even deodorants, perfumes, toothbrushes, toothpaste and hairspray. After you have dressed and made yourself beautiful in this changing room, you put on the slippers you brought with you and leave the onsen well groomed, squeaky clean and likely pink as shrimp from your "soft boil".

To be clear once again, going to the onsen is great, and not complicated at all. It is simply important to remember that you must enter the baths completely clean from head to tow. Everything else that you should do can be ascertained by discretely observing your fellow bathers.

A personal observation on shampoo and conditioner. For whatever reason, some hair products, and especially conditioner in Japan are not particularly suitable for my kind of European (Caucasian) hair. After using Japanese conditioner, my otherwise healthy hair hung from my head like overcooked spaghetti, resembling dead grass rather than the vivacious hair style I was used to. Therefore, of the products provided, it is better to use only shampoo and body soap, not conditioner. No matter where you travel in the country, your hair will thank you.

Who stinks, loses

After the onsen chapter, you can already imagine that the Japanese are sensitive to cleanliness. However, people in Japan are similarly sensitive to noise and smells.

The fact that noise is frowned upon and avoided at all costs is apparent on almost every street corner in Tokyo, for example. There are exceptions to this rule, for example at many a music-filled intersection in Shibuya or everywhere in a Don Quixote (also known as "Donki") superstore. But in general, this megacity is very quiet. Cars don't honk. People don't shout. People don't talk on the phone in public. You can even find elevated trains that run on quiet rubber tires rather than the classic screeching steel wheels.

This omnipresent silence stems from the fact that it makes it easier to live together in a crowd. True to the motto "Do unto others as you would have them do unto you," people go to great lengths to avoid being too loud. Given the countless rental apartments in the city, this makes even more sense, as their thin walls quickly turn neighbors into eavesdroppers. Even detached traditional houses demand a certain amount of acoustic consideration, since many partition walls consist only of paper-covered plywood frames.

This background should be kept in mind when traveling in Japan, especially in Japanese cities. One of the many reasons why expat families with children here like to move into compounds with numerous houses full of other non-Japanese families is that their offspring can be noisy. By noisy I mean playing soccer or tag outside with some other kids, perhaps frolicking in a wading pool in the summer. In a normal Tokyo neighborhood, unfortunately, the sounds of children playing outside can quickly invite the involvement of the neighborhood committee or even the police for disturbing the peace in the neighborhood.

Tourists have a correspondingly antisocial effect on Japanese people, for example those who talk too loudly in a restaurant, or shout loudly in the street, or even for crying one's eyes out. It's okay when you're drunk as a skunk, and even the normally reserved Japanese salaryman will bellow out into the streets. But when sober, loudness only shows a lack of education and discipline, and is generally a sign of barbarism.

The situation is similar with odor, especially body odor. Here it is actually the case that practically no one smells in Japan. You can step into a crowded subway in midsummer when the outside temperature is forty degrees. No matter how sweaty the bystanders are, none of them smells or even stinks. In a German subway, especially in summer, you often get the feeling that one of the passengers is already decomposing. That is completely unthinkable in Japan.

What is the reason for this odor-neutrality? First of all, of course, cleanliness. The majority of passengers on any metro train in Nagoya, Tokyo or Osaka took a bath the night prior, and they did so according to the same purification ritual that I described for the public onsen.

In addition, by a lucky biological coincidence (or the divine will of one of the eight-ish million Shinto gods), Japanese people produce only a very small amount of foul-smelling sweat. According to scientific studies, about seventy-five percent less than Europeans, Americans and Africans, undercut only by Chinese and Koreans.

So much for the facts. But it is also a fact that there is a very widespread scent prejudice in Japan about all foreigners, including foreigners from Korea, who, as mentioned above, actually sweat even less than Japanese themselves for biological reasons.

The prejudice is that anyone born outside Japan is more or less unclean and smells unpleasant per se. Unfortunately, many Japanese expect non-Japanese people to smell somehow annoying without even having smelt a thing. Sometimes it can be the more intense, unfamiliar scent of foreign laundry detergent like Persil or Tide that makes the surrounding passengers in the metro wrinkle their noses.

As a rule, you are not told this directly. A young Japanese friend once told me that she had met with a group of students for a game night. One of the guests had his new girlfriend with him, an exchange student from the USA. For over two hours, eight of the ten people present shared insults amongst themselves via text message that the American girl smelled unpleasantly of sweat, but no one said a word to her or her friend.

If, during a metro ride, a Japanese child nearby wrinkles his nose, runs to his parents and audibly says "kusai," you know that your own smell has been perceived as unpleasant. Whether this is due to body odor, detergent smell or perfume remains obscure. Otherwise, there is never any feedback as to what might be bothering the Japanese passengers. Nevertheless, in many subways and buses, for example, the seat next to a foreigner remains free, simply because he is recognizably a foreigner. Whether this is due to his scent, his wide hips or his foreign charisma, you will never know.

In any case, it is helpful to wash as intensively as your Japanese fellow citizens. In addition, you should bring the deodorant of your choice to Japan, because all local products fail on non-Japanese bodies, and the familiar stick-type underarm deodorant is only available far off the beaten path at Costco or on US military bases (off-limits to non-military Americans or their guests). If you now pay attention to fresh clothes, you have really done everything you can to avoid scents.

By the way, what you should not do is to apply a lot of perfume or cologne. As a rule, no or very little perfume is used in Japan. As I said, even deodorants and detergents in Japan are much more discreetly perfumed than in other countries. The goal for Japanese is the lack of any scent rather than a pleasant scent. An intense perfume or hairspray can therefore be perceived as unpleasant as body odor.

Fun fact: For some years now, sales of perfumes in Japan have been on the rise as the luxury goods industry has been promoting their fragrances as perfect gifts. This strategy seems to work to some extent, except that no one uses the contents of the pretty bottles afterwards. Instead, the bottle of Chanel No 5 is simply displayed in the bathroom after unpacking and remains there for many years as a decorative object.

By the way, one important note: in many very good restaurants perfume is actually forbidden. As a rule of thumb, I would say that the more Japanese the food, the less you should use perfume when going out. As already described, fine Japanese cuisine is about nuances, sushi is about the flawlessness of the product, the lack of smell from the fish, the subtle flavors of the rice. Here, in fact, an unexpected waft of eau de parfum would only interfere with the delicate multi-sensory experience of the meal. Many a chef therefore see it as a great sign of disrespect when his guests sit in front of him at the counter smelling strongly. Some may expel them from the premises, at least in part out of consideration for the Japanese guests sitting around them.

However, all this scent bigotry should not make you think that any intense scent is frowned upon in Japan. It's really all about body odor. For breakfast, the Japanese nevertheless happily eat their natto, fermented soybeans with the consistency of epoxy and a smell that is very reminiscent of blue cheese forgotten in a hot car. Hardly any foreigners can stand this slimy concoction, which Japanese often find very amusing. The Japanese love of natto is proof positive that customs, tastes and also the sense of smell are cultural phenomena. You have to respect them as a given, but no one should regard them as absolute.

The Japanese language

I only understand Japanese

Learning Japanese is hell.

With this short statement, one could already consider this chapter to have been dealt with conclusively and thus also end it right away. But it is generally known that Japanese is, at best, not an easy language to learn. So, let's delve a little deeper into "*nihongo*" (the name for the Japanese language, in Japanese) and its mediation.

The first concrete encounter with the Japanese language is usually in the context of a language course or in the form of a well-intentioned vocabulary list in any travel guide.

Let's first consider such a vocabulary list. As a rule, it will be a slight variation of the following words - I have taken the following overview one-to-one from a popular guide and have not changed it:

Good day/Hello - konnichi wa
Goodbye - sayonara
Yes - hai
No - iie
Thank you - arigato
Restaurant - resutoran

Using this list, we can get wonderfully into the challenges of Japanese.

The start is simple. "Hello" is "konnichiwa-." You've heard that before, and it's easy to pronounce. The "a" at the end is usually kept a little longer, so I wrote this with a hyphen.

For some reason, you also hear "*Sayonara*" quite often outside Japan, but the trouble is: In Japan, no one actually uses this word. "*Sayonara*" is used for very special, final goodbyes, with a touch of drama. When setting off on a year-long trip around the world, it fits well, also when saying goodbye to a terminally ill person.

Definitely not when leaving your hotel or a store. That's why it's best to delete "*sayonara*" from your vocabulary right away.

You can do the least wrong here with the almost always appropriate and everywhere understood "*bai bai*", which was taken one to one from English and is very common.

Yes is "*hai*", and you can use it in the same way you would the English word. Japanese would usually not let it stand alone, but still combine it with part of the question asked. "Is it raining? Yes, it's raining." Basically, though, you can't go wrong with a "*Hai!*". Colloquially, a simple, very short spoken "*uhn*", close to a light grunt is usually enough to answer almost anything in the affirmative.

"Iie" ("ee-eh") theoretically means "no", which is also correct. But this word is used quite rarely. De facto, the answer "*iie*" is rude in most cases, because it is much too direct. No one in Japan simply says "no". Only bullies do – and readers of western guidebooks, whereby once again one thing leads to another... It is better to say "no" as a sort of elongated, lilting humming sound – “mmMMm” works great. For the more advanced: *"I-eh, kekko dess(u)"* means "No, thank you," and is a simple and usually sufficiently friendly phrase to turn down or refuse an offer in a more polite situation. The "u" is, as very often in Japanese, not spoken or almost imperceptibly pronounced. As a language beginner if you just leave the “u” out, your pronunciation will already sound very good.

Next in our vocabulary list. "*Arigato*", is pronounced as it is written, and works always and everywhere as a nice "thank you". More often you will hear "*arigato gosaimass(u)*", from service staff in particular, which is more polite way of saying "thank you", and also always a good choice.

Let's move on to the last word on our list: "*Resutoran*". Didn't people joke as children that Japanese people can't pronounce "r"? Then I guess you just pronounce this word as "*Lesutolan*"? No. An r is also an r in Japanese, but it is pronounced much softer and not unlike an l. It is a sound in between r and l, a sound of its own, not simply an "l" or an “r”. What is again hardly emphasized or pronounced here, however, is the "u". As described before, it's best left out of the pronunciation. In fact, "*Resutoran*" thus reads as "*Restoran*", with a softly spoken "r". "*Lestolan*" would also be understood by everyone and is easier to pronounce if you are not sure how to pronounce a soft "r".

What do we learn from this little exercise? First of all, that the vocabulary lists in travel guides are a bit of a waste. One has the impression that someone at some point created such a list for Japanese and since then everyone has copied from this person. Neither the simplest basics of pronunciation are explained, nor are the words commonly applicable.

The solution: Either hope that after the stunning success of this book, I'll tackle the ultimate phrasebook next (which isn't very likely). Or look for some good Japanese learning podcasts and videos. These are often made with a lot of love, and there's a lot more to be gained from learning a bit of naturally spoken Japanese than from completely misleading vocabulary lists. A good start, for example, is the English-Japanese "learnjapanesepod", which you can find on all the major podcast portals, and which I really enjoyed listening to.

There is one fascinating topic that I would like to expand on here, and that is adopted words from Western languages. There are a lot of them in Japanese, far more than one would generally believe.

During the Meji Restoration beginning in 1868, Japan imported a great deal of knowledge from other countries - and with it a great deal of technical terminology. The Kingdom of Prussia served as the godfather of medicine at that time, and thus many German words found their way into the training and vocabulary of Japanese doctors. Hence, I found such beautiful loan words from German as "*gip(u)s(u)*" for plaster, "*noiroze*" for neurosis and "*his(u)teri*" for hysteria. We have also repeatedly met doctors in Japan who learned German for a few semesters as part of their studies or who studied at a German-speaking university straight away.

There are also plenty of English loan words. For example, the "*focchun kukki*", the fortune cookie. The "*f(u)raido poteto*", the fried potato or French fry. Or my favorite, the "*t(o)rab(u)r(u)*" - the trouble.

Due to the fact that all these words are reproduced in katakana, one of the Japanese syllabary scripts (more on that in a moment), they are very difficult to read and recognize despite the similar pronunciation. The only thing that helps here is to perform several translation steps in your head:

At first, as a beginner, you decipher the word itself very laboriously, and thus come from マクドナルド to "マma *クku* *ドdo* *ナna* *ルru* ド do" - "*makudonarudo*". That doesn't help you at all yet.

Now one must consider how this is probably spoken. And above all consider what all is not spoken! From this then in the first thinking step *"mak(u)donar(u)d(o)"* becomes. Now we replace the "r" by an "l": makdonald.

And, ta-da, we have ourselves the word "McDonald" (the restaurant, not the farmer)!

The flip side is that if you are a complete beginner to the language, you can completely ignore reading and writing, and will still be able to buy, for example, Western foods and many medicines in Japanese through their English, German and other Western language loan words.

What makes Japanese so difficult

Besides Japanese grammar and syntax which is simply very far removed from what most Westerners are used to, there are two other hurdles for anyone who wants to learn Japanese. These are first and foremost the ubiquitous and at first glance confusing characters, or kanjis. Then there are the levels of politeness already mentioned, which even many native Japanese do not master perfectly.

Let's start with the obvious first challenge: writing. In fact, there is more than one form of writing in Japanese: three different scripts are used in parallel. For some words in some cases Latin script is also used, so strictly speaking there are four scripts used in.

Kanji are the meat and potatoes, so to speak, of Japanese writing. They were originally Chinese characters that found their way from the mainland to the island nation around the year 600. It is a symbolic script with many thousands of characters, exactly 2,136 of which (in addition to about 10,000 vocabulary words) must be mastered in order to pass the Japanese Language Proficiency Test (JLPT) N1 test - the most widely recognized Japanese language test for Japanese language learners, comparable to the TOEFL in English. (Fun fact: These 2,136 Joyo Kanji, officially known as "standard use kanji" must be mastered by Japanese students in order for them to achieve "basic literacy" and complete middle school (grade 9) according to the Japanese Ministry of Education. So the bare minimum standard to enter Japanese high schools is the highest attainable certification for foreigners!)

The Kanji used today still correspond optically to the Chinese originals (kanjis are almost identical to the "traditional" Chinese characters still used in places like Taiwan and Singapore, but very different from than the modern "simplified" Chinese characters used in the PRC). The problem is, however, that the kanji came to Japan only after Japanese had already existed as a spoken language for thousands of years. Characters with a defined Chinese pronunciation met an existing Japanese language with completely different sounds and words.

Chinese writing AND language came to Japan via Korea, and classical Chinese became the language of the Japanese scholars. Over centuries, the Japanese saw the advantages of this Chinese script, but unfortunately its characters were not as universal as our Latin script, known by Japanese as the Roman alphabet, for the reproduction of any Japanese words. Therefore, and according to my theory because the Japanese prefer to develop proven systems instead of completely reinventing them, Japanese scholars had to assign the many thousands of Chinese characters to Japanese words pronounced as similarly as possible according to their sound. Sometimes they hit the bull's eye, most of the time, unfortunately, they didn't.

Very simply, you can think of it like this: The Germanic people decide to adopt English kanji as their script. There is a kanji in English with the pronunciation "house" - perfect, the Germanic people henceforth use this kanji for their word "Haus", which translates 1:1 into the English term “house”. There is also an English kanji with the pronunciation "post", which means a post for the British. The Teutons also adopt this kanji, but with them it now means "post office". Thus, British and Germanic people can both correctly understand the kanji "Haus / house", but the Germanic kanji for "post office" is read by British visitors as "fence post".

The result of this process in Japan can be seen today in the fact that about seventy percent of the two thousand most commonly used kanji have at least two readings. A Japanofied way of saying the old Chinese, because this was preserved by the Japanese and is still used today, and in addition the new Japanese reading. Sometimes there are even different Japanese readings. One of the most universal kanjis, 生 which stands for "life," (among other possible, but related, meanings) has a whopping thirteen different readings. Depending on its context, it is used to convey e.g. life, living, birth, growth, raw (uncooked) food, food waste and, most importantly, draft beer.

All of this makes kanji in Japanese extremely complex. Add to this the fact that every schoolchild must be able to write all the kanji by hand, and it becomes a little easier to understand why many Japanese children take extra lessons in reading and writing so early, and then over many years of evening and weekend classes. The complexity of their native language deprives them of almost any opportunity to engage more broadly or deeply with subjects other than learning and cramming on just how to read and write.

The beauty is that by learning kanji, you can really delve deep into Japanese thinking and worldview. Through the different readings of a kanji, often combined with the beauty and expressiveness of calligraphy, Japanese poetry can be very complex, elegantly simple and downright magical. At the same time, it is only through learning kanji that one understands how imprecise Japanese is, at least grammatically. Many references are only revealed by the context of a sentence, and even personal pronouns like "I" and "you" are not written, but must be understood by the reader. This simultaneously puts the onus of ensuring that the context is properly understood squarely on the shoulders of the writer.

Hiragana is an ancient Japanese phonetic script originally derived mostly from Chinese characters that can be used to write basically any Japanese word. The vast majority of characters represent a syllable, not a single sound. There are the vowels a, i, e, o and u, but beyond that only syllables: ka, sa, ta, na, ki, si, chi, ni, and so on. Consonants, with the exception of "n", always stand before a vowel. This makes many Japanese words quite long, and unfortunately, they often sound similar. Here I would like to remind you of my example with “Tonkatsu” and “Kotatsu”, pork schnitzel and heated coffee table, which I mixed up for two years.

The great thing about hiragana is that there are only forty-six of them. With that, plus some easy-to-learn attributes similar to dots on ä, ü, and ö, you can write any Japanese word accurately.

The problem is that you need a lot of hiragana compared to kanji. To take a particularly long example: "rules", "government" or even "religious festival" is called *Matsurigoto*. This can be written in hiragana as まつりごと. Or simply as kanji: 政.

Katakana originate from the attempt to simplify hiragana. In fact, they are also easier to paint with a brush or write with a pen, because they are more reduced and straightforward than hiragana. However, because of the reduction, they are also less unique, and therefore easy to confuse with each other. The straighter and tighter Katakana are not any easier to learn or read than hiragana, their more rotund siblings. Katakana are used almost exclusively to write foreign words. For example, the aforementioned fast-food chain from the United States, makudonarudo. In hiragana, this word would look like this: まくどなるど. However, it is actually written exclusively in katakana: マクドナルド.

Now we come to the important politeness levels of the Japanese language. These also exist in some European languages, but people probably think about them less often. Of course, it also makes a difference here whether one says "I am infinitely sorry to disturb you while you are chewing. Would you mind passing me the bread at the next opportunity? That would be very nice." Or just "Pass me the bread." However, we would turn a blind eye to children and language beginners if the level of politeness is not perfect. And even with native speakers, it is more a question of situation, mood and upbringing how politely they communicate.
In Japanese, however, the levels of politeness are immovably cemented. Depending, for example, on the age of the speaker, their social position, their degree of kinship, and some more.

In some cases, the constellation of speakers even results in levels of politeness that may even differ on both sides of the dialogue.

For people who did not grow up in Japan, it is very challenging to get into the correct level here. And even many Japanese people find it very difficult to always choose the correct level.

In addition, there are not only formal levels of politeness, but also codified ways of conversing. Anyone who deviates from this is at least conspicuous - and, depending on the context, is also considered impolite, because this breaks the harmony of a normal conversation (which always starts and ends in the same way). In concrete terms, very specific phrases are expected at various points, especially in greetings in stores, when dealing with distant acquaintances, on the telephone and so on, which all those involved reel off without thinking much about it. But their absence confuses everything.

If we, as foreigners with a painstakingly memorized vocabulary, at least occasionally manage to actually use one of the specific phrases expected in this context in an everyday situation, a ping-pong dialogue can develop as if by itself, in which almost every utterance of the counterpart is repeated for reassurance, and which takes place almost automatically, as if according to an unconscious script of successive, identical questions and polite phrases for the specific situation that has been internalized by everyone. This can be extremely inspiring at times. And it can replenish the necessary frustration tolerance buffers for the next lost-in-translation moment that is sure to come soon, when the magic trigger formula is simply not known or has once again slipped your mind.

The sequence of resuming what has been said, the predictability of the next utterance, and the silent agreement on the course of the conversation can then feel like a dance - according to rules internalized by all participants. Like dancing, you just have to know these very rules well so that you don't step on your (conversational) partner's toes.

The only chance to learn this is to practice, practice, practice. And to mingle again and again with great passion with your Japanese acquaintances in Tokyo dancing elegantly around you as if in silent unison, hoping that the concentrated counting of beats cannot be read directly from your lips.

Language lessons of horror

I have already described how important education is in Japan. This is especially true for the Japanese language and its characters, which Japanese people spend many years of their lives learning. This importance, the high demands on the students and the associated rigor is transferred from normal schools in Japan to Japanese language courses for foreigners. There was no exception to this in my entire circle of acquaintances in Japan, regardless of whether it was instruction at private language schools, state language institutes or individual lessons.

Lessons always followed the same pattern, in the same sequence of steps and with the same high emphasis on politeness - and unfortunately also with the same little reference to the use of language in everyday life. It is very important to the teachers that their students do not insult anyone in formal interactions due to a lack of language skills - and potentially bring shame on the sensei. Therefore, one is taught a very confident, polite, but unfortunately not very practical Japanese. The Japanese that has been painstakingly crammed in over many hours is thus far removed from real life. Because in pubs and supermarkets, Japanese is no more complex than most other languages in the world. Language teachers, however, do not take this into consideration and unfortunately fill the brains of their customers with a lot of polite phrases and constructions. Although one could survive quite well without these.

My teacher, a lovely lady of about seventy, kindly but strictly refused to teach me colloquial Japanese. It always gave the impression that I had asked her to do something grossly improper. Whenever I asked about a phrase I had heard in the office or after work in town, she would just laugh sheepishly, look uncomfortably at the table in front of her - and continue with the lesson we were in. Sometimes, after the embarrassed laughter, she would say that what I had just quoted should not be used that way. And that was the end of the subject. All the foreigners with whom

I have spoken about Japanese lessons have had this experience, or something very similar. You can't fight it, and the student has to go through the deep valley of very polite Japanese before he is finally allowed to order a beer with just a few words.

I'll illustrate this with a very concrete example from my time in Japan. After a few weeks of intensive Japanese lessons, I was able to proudly order my beer in the pub in the evening: "*Nama biru o ippai onegaishimasu*". "*Nama biru*" is beer on tap, "*onegaishimasu*" I already explained and means "please". "*Ippai*" a contraction of the Japanese word for "one" or "*ichi*", and the counter "*hai*", which in this case counts the number of poured drinks.

However, there are lots of different counting words in Japanese, and the correct use depends on the geometric shape of the object to be counted, or even what kind it is. There are different counting words for flat or cylindrical objects, for small animals, for large animals, for houses, for books, for chapters in these books, and many different things. It is a nightmare for every Japanese language student to commit these to memory. Like several other aspects of the Japanese language, fluency with counters comes more with time and experience using the language, than it does from traditional study.

In the case of my beer, I chose the counter for drinks. And that is called "*ippai*" in the case of ONE drink. This then becomes "*nihai*" in the case of two beers. And in case of three beers "*sanbon*". You can probably imagine how long it took me to be able to correctly count various things from one to ten, much to the delight of my teacher. And to remember more than a hundred different counting words, which, to top it all off, always had some kind of irregularity.

But back to my beer in the pub. Concentrated, I recited my sentence there, my team was very impressed and clapped because of my perfect Japanese, and I was very proud. Then my colleagues ordered.

"*Nama*."

"Nama mo hitotsu."

"Nama mittsu, onegaishimasu."

And then a few glasses of wine, I save us here.

What I learned here, my teacher would never have taught me. But it was to accompany me through all the bars in Japan for the next few years. Just "*Nama*" is pretty crude, but it always works. It gets you a beer on tap. Younger Japanese (after a few beers, older ones too...) order supplies that way.

"*Nama mo hitotsu*" means "one more beer on tap." "*Hitotsu*" is a kind of wildcard singular count word, used to mean "one general inanimate object". It's not particularly elegant, polite and specific, but this counter on the ending "tsu" can count pretty much any non-living thing and any form and is always understood everywhere.

"*Nama mittsu, onegaishimasu*", the order of the third colleague, simply means "Three draft beers, please". "*Mittsu*" is the standard counter for "three" here.

So if you want to spend some time in Japan, but don't want to become a native there, save your time and money and forgo formal language lessons. It is better to find good podcasts and websites (I found tofugu.com very helpful), in the very best case a Japanese speaking person in your personal environment for short dialogue trainings, and rather learn some essential, colloquial phrases and expressions than awkward phrases and vocabulary. At the elementary level one reaches by doing this, no one in Japan expects advanced use of politeness levels. So one retains one's linguistic foolishness. And yet, if you can speak a little more at this practical level than the many silent foreigners who can't utter more than "*arrigato,*" you'll get to know a lot more about the country and its people.

However, if you consciously decide to take a real language course because you find the language fascinating, want to understand anime in the original or even live in Japan for a longer period of time, then you should approach this adventure with a lot of verve and a fair amount of humility. An arduous journey lies ahead, which offers little sense of achievement, especially in its first sections. The deeper you go, however, the more a large part of Japanese culture is deciphered through the language and its complexity, which makes more and more sense.

There is an exciting change in the way Japanese people interact with you as you become more fluent in Japanese. At the beginning, when you can just speak a few very formal sentences and many vocabulary words are simply missing, every counterpart in Japan is extremely indulgent. They are happy that a foreigner is learning Japanese, motivate you with their smiles, and praise your great progress again and again. As described above, my first formally correct beer order led to applause from my team present - although the sentence was terribly stiff and mechanical.

But if you then exceed a certain level, such as that of the lowest official language level JLPT N5 after about a hundred hours of lessons, this changes massively. Suddenly you are constantly being corrected. Colleagues shake their heads and ask you to express what you just said more precisely. Japanese friends suddenly correct you in dialogues. According to reports, even Japanese spouses in mixed marriages switch to strict correction mode once they reach a certain level, pointing out to their partner every incorrect level of politeness and every inaccurate expression. An entire people becomes teachers as if at the push of a button.

My wife and I have made this observation ourselves, but have also heard it from many friends. My theory is that Japanese children are treated in a similar way, and that this is why all our counterparts unconsciously behaved in almost the same way. Up to a certain basic level there is praise and motivation. And then the collective switches to strict teaching mode, which the whole nation has had to go through for many generations in order to learn to master its complex language world.

Bonus for those who want to learn even more about Japan

Book and film tips

For those who want to learn even more about Japan, but do not want to wait until the sequel to this book comes out, I recommend the following books and films. It is a very colorful mixture that conveys the diversity of Japanese culture and society, as well as modern Japanese (social) history in an entertaining way.

Tampopo, *film*
Tampopo was made in 1985 by the director Juzo Itami, who is highly revered in Japan. The film tells a wild, crazy and in some places disturbing story about Japan's unconditional will to perfection - in the preparation of ramen noodles. In narrative style and visuals a true Italo-Western including cowboy hats in the Japanese province, the good 120 minutes of arthouse film feel like a mixture of various Tarantino films, Natural Born Killers, Monty Python and a soft porn. At the same time, the film not only gives you a sense of the truly boundless perfectionism of Japanese chefs, but also a glimpse into the wild and creative times during the Bubble Economy.

Juzo Itami is no longer alive, by the way. He fell from the sixth floor of a skyscraper in 1997 while he was working on a film about the yakuza...

Spirited Away, *movie*
This very atmospheric anime by Hayao Miyazaki has won more awards than any other animated film, including an Oscar. The story takes place for the most part in a hotel traditional inn featuring a huge sento, a Japanese bathhouse (specifically a bathhouse in which the water is not naturally heated, separating it from onsen, which we covered in this book). The special thing about this special bathhouse hotel, run by a witch, is that only ghosts are permitted within the property. Thus, every evening a seemingly endless procession of various nature spirits moves into

the sento, where they are waited upon by other mythical creatures and by the heroine Chihiro.

In magnificent images, you are immersed in this mystical world full of Shinto deities and spirits, encounter metaphors on the brutalization of Japanese culture (according to reports, the director also criticizes Western influences here), as well as the increasing pollution and disregard for Japan's nature, filled with Shinto deities. In addition, there are unique characters, the entertaining adventures of the main character Chihiro and a dense, haunting atmosphere that completely captivates you for a good two hours.

Demon Slayer, ***TV series and movie***

Demon Slayer swept Japan during the coronavirus pandemic and became a real hit in just a few months. A feature film, which continues the story of the TV series from the end of the first season, Mugen Train, became the most commercially successful animated film of all time and, due partially to Japan being one of the only countries in the world running cinemas during that wave of the coronavirus pandemic, was the world's highest grossing film of 2020!

In Demon Slayer, set in a fantasy version of Japan at the turn of the 19th century, or around the Taisho era, you accompany the boy Tanjiro, a young charcoal maker's son, on his way to becoming a demon hunter. He is accompanied by some close friends and his sister, who he is trying to save in spite of her recent (stunted) transformation into a demon. Sound like a classic fantasy story? It is. But then better told, more surprising and more exciting than many other representatives of this genre. In addition, there are wonderful landscapes, moods, buildings and visual effects, many of them previously unseen in animated films and very imaginatively created.

I saw "Mugen Train," in a sold-out IMAX theater in Tokyo and was surrounded by laughing, sobbing, cheering and unrestrained crying people who were so moved by the story of Tanjiro and, in this case, the death of a major character, as I have never experienced in an animated film. Great cinema!

Pachinko, ***book and series***

Pachinko is a great book absolutely worth reading by the Korean author Min Jin Lee. However, I would like to recommend the TV series created by Apple TV. The plot, though told slightly differently, is largely the same as the novel. A Korean family is accompanied over three generations and about 80 years on their life - from a small Korean fishing village to Tokyo, through two world wars, the Japanese occupation of Korea and the many problems of the Korean population of Japan after the war until today.

In Japan, the book and series have been negatively criticized for being hostile to Japan. In fact, many of the fictional events in the life of the Korean family are told from the Korean point of view, dealing with the issues of oppression, mistreatment and later disrespect of Koreans by Japan. However, Korean friends of mine confirmed that similar stories were experienced in their families. At the same time, the period of Japanese occupation of Korea and parts of China during World War II has not been critically examined in Japan to the present day and is meagerly reviewed in Japanese school history lessons.

Thus, this magnificently produced, visually stunning and in many scenes beautiful series not only provides unique insights into historical scenes from Japan and Korea, but also into a suppressed part of Japanese history.

Tokyo Underworld, ***book***

A quite magnificent book about the reconstruction of Japan after the Second World War, the emergence of today's Japanese society and political culture in Japan embedded in the hair-raising biography of the American Nick Zapetti. Robert Whiting's book traces Zapetti's life as part of Japan's occupation forces, as a bootlegger, and as the operator of one of Tokyo's most successful nightclubs. His story is tightly interwoven with the yakuza, sumo wrestlers and American intelligence operatives.

The book was written 20 years ago and has been largely forgotten, but it is a must read for anyone interested in Japan.

Tokyo Vice, *book and TV series*

My third non-fiction book tip covers Japan's recent history. Jake Adelstein came to Tokyo as a young American, studied Japanese, and in 1993 became the first ever foreign beat reporter at the Yomiuri Shimbun (Shimbun meaning newspaper), the world's largest-circulation daily newspaper and a center-right staple of Japanese journalism. Just reading how he found his way to the Yomiuri and took his first steps as a journalist in the remote suburbs outside Tokyo is worth buying the book.

Things get really exciting and educational when Adelstein returns to Tokyo and begins to do research on human trafficking and prostitution in the Japanese capital.

At the end of the thoroughly tragic story, Adelstein has to flee Japan. In his very entertaining narration of the events from the early 2000s, one learns a lot about life, work, relationships and the omnipresent yakuza in present-day Tokyo, in addition to the actual criminal story he uncovered at the time.

The TV and streaming video adaptation of his book was released as a series on HBO in 2022. The book is definitely more profound and educational, but the series is also fun and highly recommended.

Adelstein himself still writes for various newspapers today, and his very well-researched, comprehensive articles, for example for the English-language Japan Times, are well worth reading. He has also repeatedly appeared as a vocal critic of the assassinated former prime minister Shinzo Abe, which many people in Japan resent. Some of his articles on this subject are worth reading and can be found on the Internet using the usual search engines.

Rice, Noodle, Fish, *book*

Matt Goulding, award-winning food journalist, sets out on a journey through Japan. Over 5,000 kilometers, he meets chefs, farmers, food lovers, Michelin-starred chefs, and ramen shop operators, all of whom he introduces and describes in a very readable reportage style.

This book blurs the categories, it teaches the reader a great deal about Japan without being a travel guide, it imparts great knowledge about Japanese cuisine without being a restaurant guide, and it lets you delve deep into Japanese society without being a cultural guide.

Extremely entertaining and at the same time very respectful, the author describes his experiences from Hokkaido to Okinawa, a great mix of information and inspiration. In addition, there are plenty of atmospheric photos that make you want to jump on the plane the very next day and fly to Japan.

Made in the USA
Las Vegas, NV
20 July 2024

92668752R00135